~Daughters of the Most High~

Why Smart Girls do Dumb Things

And The God Who Loves Them

~Daughters of the Most High~

Why Smart Girls do Dumb Things

And The God Who Loves Them

Nakilah Shannon

Judah House Press

Unless otherwise indicated, all Scripture quotations are from the New International Version. Copyright © 1973, 1978, 1984, International Bible Society. Used by permission.

Scripture quotations marked MSG are from The Message: The Bible in Contemporary English, copyright © 1993, 1994, 1995, 1996, 2000, 2001, 2002. Used by permission of NavPress Publishing

Scripture quotations marked KJV are from the King James Version of the Bible

Scripture quotations marked NKJV are from New King James Version of the Bible, copyright © 1979, 1980, 1982 by Thomas Nelson, Inc., publishers.

Copyright © 2015 by Nakilah Shannon

ISBN 13: 978-0692570241

ISBN 10: 0692570241

All rights reserved. This book or parts thereof may not be reproduced in any form, stored in a retrieval system, or transmitted in any form by any means (electronic, mechanical, photocopy, recording, or otherwise), without prior permission in writing from the copyright owner.

Judah House Press
P.O. Box 55472
Indianapolis, Indiana 46205
judahhousepress.com

This book was printed in the United States of America

Contents

Foreword	vii
Acknowledgments	xi
Introduction	1
Eve	7
Mrs. Lot	17
The Lot Ladies	25
Leah	37
Rachel	51
Sarah	61
Tamar	71

Foreword

Oftentimes, people get caught in the act while committing a crime. At times, these crimes can be something as simple as shoplifting in a retail store, to a heinous crime like assault and battery or even murder. In this digital and technological age, there may be a video of the person caught in the act or even better, an audio recording of them conversing about the crime. Yet after being caught and put on trial, a good lawyer with the evidence stacked against their client, will still attempt to sway the judge or jury's decision towards not guilty. Not saying their client didn't do the crime because that part was obvious; however, in the act of doing the crime, they suggest they were "temporarily insane." In other words, for that moment of reckless behavior, they were out of their mind, not thinking rationally and unable to reason the difference between truth and reality. However, others would keep it simple, and call it what it was – that was just DUMB!

Remarkably, there are some people who are actually declared "not guilty" because of this momentary mental meltdown which, when supported by a psychiatric evaluation that substantiates the possibility of temporary insanity, can influence a judge and jury to move towards an acquittal. They walk away a free person, absolved from all penalties associated with the crime they got caught committing.

Now, let's wake up to reality and deal with the fact that it's not that simple. If we would be very honest with ourselves, most of us would like to consider ourselves smart enough to make rational and mature life decisions. Yet at the same time, have to agree there are times that if the stars line up perfectly and the people I have around me say the right or wrong thing at the precise time the moon is full or during a solar eclipse, we are prone to expose our perfect imperfections by being smart enough to do dumb things… not realizing or better yet ignoring the results – painful, undesired consequences that have the emotional power to produce a ripple effect on our present lives and future relationships for many years to come.

Most likely, you are reading this book because you are curious about a topic that resonates with your current state of living or that situation you think nobody knows about. You know the one that is hidden in the back of your mental closet, right behind guilt and shame. I don't blame you! If you ever want to live a healthy life, you must figure this thing out that has been tormenting you throughout your life. Admit it; you want relief, not tomorrow but RIGHT NOW!

The challenge is, you know you're smart, but you also know you occasionally do dumb things. Is that even possible? ***"I'm smart but I do dumb things!"*** – YES!

Although this statement is an oxymoron (two contradictory terms that appear in a conjunction), smart/dumb, it still rings true.

Personally, I can't say I've seen it all, but I certainly have seen enough over 20 years of ministry. As a pastor, life coach and counselor, I must admit, I consistently see this scenario played out all the time and mostly more so in the lives of women than men. This includes many types of women: educated, beautiful, independent, successful, entrepreneurs, business executives, preachers, housewives, single mothers, and so on. I've seen them doing things, making decisions, and connecting with certain people that they know are not good for them, yet doing it anyway. Under the circumstances, I have to ask the proverbial question that this book looks to answer, **"Why do Smart girls do Dumb Things?"**

I am grateful that there is a woman who has truly heard from God regarding this subject, Nakilah Shannon. She has tackled this issue with poise and a prowess beyond her years – Only God could have spoken so clearly on a subject that has been so damaging to so many women for so long.

I can assure you, **"Why do Smart girls do Dumb Things"** not only answers the question, but it will also heal your heart from the brokenness and bitterness that have been eating away at your soul from the inside out, freeing you from the inability to love and be loved.

Through this book, God has used Nakilah's transparency to be the prescription glasses you need to see Him in your situation. It's her humility that has afforded her the wisdom of a skilled surgeon graced by the hand of God. Like you, she has survived the consequences of her own painful pitfalls and using the word of God, meticulously breaks down the strongholds women face, exposing the roots that have been breeding confusion for generations in your present and past, but not for your future.

Get ready for the first time in your life to actually see clearly, with no fogginess. Get ready to recognize who you are by discovering who you are not. Get ready to graduate to the next level by discovering why your God given purpose has been held hostage by hostile living, all because you couldn't answer one question ***"Why do Smart girls do Dumb things?"***

Get ready, for a journey through this powerful book that won't end until you have reached your God appointed destiny, and at the same time, helping other smart women along the way to be free from doing dumb things. **#EnjoyTheRide**

Steve Bozeman
Sr. Pastor, New Beginnings Church of Atlanta
Author, Your Problems Have Purpose
Atlanta, GA.

Acknowledgments

I want to take some time to thank some special people. The first is my Heavenly Father. Thank you Lord for equipping me to complete this project. Thank you for loving me through ALL the dumb choices I've made and for keeping me through the foolishness and issues. Lord I am nothing without you. Thank you for blessing me with the opportunity to be a blessing to my sisters. I am fully confident that you are going to bless my sisters through this book. It is appointed and anointed for such a time as this. I pray they receive it in Jesus name and it edifies and encourages them to be the women they are called to be.

Thank you always to my dear friend and Brother Larry Gilkey. I appreciate you and love you and your family from the bottom of my heart. Thank you for all that you do.

Special thanks to Pastor Steve Bozeman, my spiritual father and mentor. I can't begin to explain what you mean to me. Your ministry has saved me years of bad decisions and your Abba (fatherly) love has truly been a reflection of God's fatherly love for me. Thank you for helping me grow through the hard times and loving me through the dumb ones. You're forever stuck with me and I'm forever grateful to God for your tough love and direction.

Thank you Trease Sears for being my accountability partner. I appreciate you.

To my family and friends. My daughters who helped me keep up with "The Book". I appreciate you little ladies and I pray that even through my imperfections you see the perfect love of God. I'm always grateful for my mother. To my other family and friends, thank you for your encouragement. Aunt Tam for always being more excited than me! Chalice for helping me write the summary, and Amanda for doing the editing.

Thank you to the countless bad choices… you weren't bad people, just bad for me. Thank you for leaving and letting me go not matter how much I fought it at the time. I appreciate you letting me go, because it was in my quiet times with God, crying over situations like you, that I realized that even though I'm a smart girl who's made some really dumb choices, God still loves me. Thank you for being a vessel.

Nakilah Shannon
~Daughter of the Most High~

Introduction

We've all seen her before. She's smart, beautiful and educated. She's a boss in the board room, handles her business at home, and keeps herself up. From the outside looking in, she is one smart woman. So, why is it she makes some of the dumbest choices? Let's be honest, sometimes that woman is us. We are book smart, street smart, a "go to" type of leader, but when it comes to certain areas of our lives, we find ourselves making the dumbest decisions. At the end of the day, there is one major, undeniable reason that Daughters of the Most High, very smart women, can make very dumb choices. It's because they don't trust God! It took me years of errors, mistakes, prayers and several dumb choices to understand this. It was ever so clear when God spoke this into my spirit; that I was coming out of a very dumb season. It was a season in my life where, in certain areas, I was highly effective and in others, I was failing miserably. It's like when you get a cold spell in the middle of the summer; I had overlapping seasons. So in the areas where I needed improvement, I was making some really dumb and horrible choices; choices that may have been understandable for a younger woman in her early twenties, but just plain foolishness for a woman in her mid-thirties. And don't judge me; plenty of us have stories to tell. One of the most popular television shows today is based off of this very line…Scandal. We shut down everything on Thursday nights, the kids know not to ask for anything, the phone better not ring, and we flood Facebook and social media with play by play highlights of what Olivia Pope has going on. But let's take a step back and really look at Ms. Pope. She is a powerhouse when it comes to handling business. When she has the white hat on, she doesn't play; she's fierce, upfront, and ruthless and would do what it takes to get the job done. She's also a mistress, (a side chick). Her main love is a married man and she can't shake him loose. She falls for his tricks and schemes and even when she tries to date someone else, she always finds herself back in his arms. She's a prime example of a modern day smart girl doing dumb things. The tragedy is we celebrate her and her choices while overlooking her indiscretions for the sake of entertainment.

As we take a journey through explaining this phenomenon, we will look at some of our own sisters who had all the potential in the world to make a wise choice, but because of their lack of trust in God, they missed the mark and paid a steep price. We will also look at how we make some of the same choices and what we can do to avoid falling into the same pitfalls.

The purpose of this book is to take an honest look at ourselves. It's not to condemn or belittle, but to have the courage to look our flaws in the eye and resolve to fix them. We've all heard that we can't fix what we don't face. The enemy hopes we continue to overlook our flaws and only focus on our strengths. Yes, we should find ways to celebrate our success, but we are only as strong as our weakest link. We can spend years building these great empires and reputations but our dumb mistakes can ruin a lifetime of work. It can ruin our credibility, reputation, relationships, and our resources. The world is not as forgiving as God. One minute they will cheer Hosanna and "crucify her" the next.

No woman is an island and our decisions don't just affect us, they also affect those around us as well. Our families, friends, and colleagues are affected by our decisions. If you're anything like me, you'll realize that there are complete strangers waiting for your wise choices and are negatively affected by your poor choices. Someone else's breakthrough is waiting on your obedience and mine. My first book was based off of the positive lessons learned from years of bad choices. But had I never stepped out and resolved to make some better choices, others would still be in bondage. This book is the same way. It took a lot of dumb choices to get here. Praise be to God that some smart ones followed.

Our actions and words are our reality; it's how we are perceived. It's time that all areas of our lives look like our most successful ones. Will we be perfect? Of course not, but we will be productive in all areas. We will not be bosses in the boardroom but bound to unproductive relationships. We can't be amazing in ministry but a mess in our finances. I can only speak for myself when I say; many of my mistakes came in the form of a relationship. I can make great choices when it comes to business. I'd like to think that I'm pretty smart as well, both book and street. I even have a firm grasp of the elusive "common sense", but show me a fine man, regardless of his issues, and I'll show you my foolish side. In the words of singer and song writer, Taylor Swift, "You look like my next MISTAKE." I would throw all common sense out of the door, until I finally trusted God. I realized I made several of my mistakes from a place of fear and lack of trust in God, I didn't trust God or His process. I believed He had forgotten about me in that area, until it was time for Him to bail me out of it. I can't tell you how long this book has been in my spirit; how long it's been sitting there waiting to be birthed, but it couldn't happen until I, myself, stopped being a smart girl making dumb choices. Praise be to God for loving me in spite of me and my bad choices.

Maybe relationships aren't your kryptonite, maybe its money, health or friendship. Whatever it is, it's holding you back from greatness. It's keeping you from the fullness of God. Trusting God sounds like too simple of a solution, but it's powerful. Many of us feel we already do, but if we look back over our past and really review some of our dumb choices, we will see that we were not trusting God. If we did it from a place of fear, that's not trusting God; from a place of shame, again not trusting God. Trusting God at His word brings us to a place of peace, even when it doesn't look like trusting Him is beneficial, but if we hold to it we finally realize that "all things actually worked together for our good" (Romans 8:28). My prayer is that you stick in it with me and get to the heart of your issues, that you set your life straight and the enemy as well. He doesn't think you will be willing to put in the work. He thinks you'll be like those guys we run into from high school from years ago or a one hit wonder. You know the type, all they have are those "back in the day" highlight stories or only one or two well-known songs. That's what happens with us when we only focus on our few successes but fail to spend time on our issues. Remember, Satan was wise and beautiful and it took ONLY ONE dumb mistake, thinking he was better than God, and it caused him to miss the blessings of God. Don't fall to the same fate. Don't miss all that God has for you because you are a smart girl making a dumb choice. Get all that your loving God has for you.

Eve

In the beginning

Genesis 3:1-6
Now the serpent was craftier than any of the wild animals the LORD God had made. He said to the woman, "Did God really say, 'You must not eat from any tree in the garden'?" The woman said to the serpent, "We may eat fruit from the trees in the garden, ³ but God did say, 'You must not eat fruit from the tree that is in the middle of the garden, and you must not touch it, or you will die.'" "You will not certainly die," the serpent said to the woman. ⁵ "For God knows that when you eat from it your eyes will be opened, and you will be like God, knowing good and evil." When the woman saw that the fruit of the tree was good for food and pleasing to the eye, and also desirable for gaining wisdom, she took some and ate it. She also gave some to her husband, who was with her, and he ate it.

Here we have our sister Eve. Ah Eve... you started out with so much amazing potential. God created you to be a helpmate to Adam. With all He had created it still wasn't right in the world until He fashioned you. Adam adored you and the enemy envied you. You were on your way to greatness. As we look at Eve we see the first example of a smart woman doing a dumb thing.

Eve's Smart Move

She knows God's word and is confident enough to repeat it in the face of the enemy. In verse 3:3 Eve responds to the enemies question with the word of God. She recited it back to the serpent the same way she received it from God. Eve even gave her reply with confidence in the word she had received. She didn't waiver in the beginning, she said " God did say" it reminds me of Jesus when he was tempted after His 40 days of fasting and praying He combatted the temptations of the enemy by using the word of God, Eve did the same thing.

Eve was also fashioned, shaped, molded, designed, and created by the very hands of God. Created in His image, she was designed by the best, so it's no question that God had deposited even just a little bit of wisdom in our sister. Although her next move isn't the brightest, her first move lets us know she had the potential for wisdom.

Eve's Not So Smart Move

Eve knew Gods word, she even repeated it to the enemy so we know she was aware. Her not so bright move was when she started to believe the word of the enemy over the Word of God. There had to be some level of ignorance on Eve's part. She recited God's command word for word but somehow the enemy was still able to convince her, pretty easily I might mention, that there was an error in what God had said. She stated God CERTAINLY said "eat of the fruit and you will die. He didn't say if it was spiritual, physical or, emotional, He just said die. At this stage of the game, it's not 100% clear to me if she really knew the whole concept of death. Maybe she had witnessed some of the animals die but didn't truly understand the concept. The commandment to not eat the fruit came second hand. The command came in 2:17 but Eve wasn't created until 2:21-22, and there is no more mention of God giving the orders not to eat of the tree. In fact the very next chapter starts with the serpent coming to deceive Eve. I wonder if Eve asked any questions when Adam gave her the "rules" of the garden, did she clarify what "die" really meant? Did Adam explain God to her and how He has so generously given EVERYTHING else, and that even though the fruit on THAT TREE looks tasty there are 100's of other pieces of fruit that taste just as good. Well your guess is as good as mine, but what I do know is there was some type of space left for the enemy to slither his way in. This was the world's very first dumb move by a smart woman.

In verse 3:6 Eve stopped listening to the Word of God because of the word of the enemy and let her eyes write a check the rest of the world would have to cash. It wasn't actually until Adam ate of the fruit that the world changed as they knew it, but it's very clear that Eve had strong influence over Adam. She didn't have to beg or plead she simply "gave" (6: b) and Adam set the world on a path to sin. From this one decision, one dumb move, all of mankind fell into the life of sin. Adam and Eve were kicked out of the garden. God had provided everything in the garden, stable employment, protection, provisions, direct access to Him. He had provided freedom from shame and guilt. There was no judgment in the garden. They were able to roam about freely naked and unashamed.

All of that was lost due to choosing what we see over what God said. Eve trusted the word of a snake that had not provided anything or wasn't protecting her, had no part in her creation and wellbeing but somehow she was convinced he knew better than God… hmmmm sound familiar? It definitely should. How many of us are guilty of this. God's word says we are His; we are fearfully and wonderfully made (Psalm 139:14). His word says we were made in His image (Genesis 1:27) and that He has plans for us, and not just any kind of plans, but prosperous plans (Jeremiah 29:11), plans that are designed to help us and not harm us. God has forgiven our sins (1 John1:9) and created in us clean hearts and right spirits (Psalm 51:10). He has even promised to work all things out for our good (Romans 8:28). He even loved us so much He gave Jesus as a sacrifice for our sins (John 3:16). With all of this and more, it takes just one snake to come along and change the game. This snake didn't do any of the things for you that God did or even care about your future, yet this one conversation with him negates everything in you that God said. You begin to question everything God's Word said. Who you are, your purpose, His plans and love for you. Everything comes under fire and as soon as the enemy sees that space he swoops in and begins the deception. Let's clear something up before we go any further. The enemy comes to steal, kill and destroy. Not to just upset you or hurt your feelings, but to kill your dreams, steal your joy and destroy your future. This is why we can't give him any space. Eve did and let's look at what happened as a result.

Eve

The Consequences of Eve's Actions

1. She caused her husband to sin although he was the head, he trusted her decision. Verse 6 says he was with her but I'm not sure if he truly knew, wasn't paying attention, was too mesmerized by her beauty. I don't know what was going on that we didn't read, but Adam never spoke up. If he did know or if he didn't he trusted her and ate of the fruit along with her. This threw him into the path of sin.

2. Once this happened they were now subject to shame and embarrassment (3:7). This is not what God had intended for them. He had designed it so they could be fully exposed and unashamed. The eating of the fruit ruined this. This caused them to hide form God (3:8). So now the shame has caused them to hide from God... isn't that exactly how we do? We sin against God, find ourselves covered in sin, and then hide from God. We hide because we don't want to face the reality of what we've done.

3. The decision then caused dissention between the couple. In 3:12 Adam has gone from calling Eve "bone of his bone" to "that woman" and he quickly threw her under the bus trying to avoid punishment. After God watches everybody pointing fingers, He then hands out the punishment. Adam will have to work hard for what use to be provided with ease. In the garden his work was pleasurable but after the fall it becomes punishment. Eve had to endure the pain of child birth and her desire is now unto her husband, and now he's to rule over her. Then in an effort to protect the tree God had to banish Adam and Eve from the garden.

4. From this seemingly smart woman's one dumb decision, her family suffered and so did the rest of the world. This is a powerful lesson to us. Our decisions

don't just affect us, but our families and our communities as well. Others are watching whether we like it or not. With that being said, are we expected to be perfect? God no! That's not the intention of this book. We are only expected to grow and mature in our decision making.

Lessons from Sister Eve

We can be knowledgeable in the things of God and still believe the lies of the enemy. We show a lack of trust by going against the word of God. We give the enemy that little bit of space and he wiggles his way right on in. How can I keep from making the same mistakes? I'm glad you asked.

1. Learn the word of God for yourself. 2 Timothy 2:15

[15] Study to shew thyself approved unto God, a workman that needeth not to be ashamed, rightly dividing the word of truth.

2 Timothy 2:15 (KJV)

As I alluded to earlier I wonder if Eve got the commandment second hand. It doesn't say that God told her directly. I don't see why Eve couldn't have gone to God herself. Even when the enemy said "God didn't say…" she could have easily said "Um God, can you come here for a second? I need some clarity." Well so can we; through prayer and reading His word we can gain clarity and understanding about what God says when the enemy comes and begins to spit his lies. Know the word for yourself.

2. Hide the Word in your heart Psalm 119:11

¹¹ Thy word have I hid in mine heart, that I might not sin against thee.

Psalm 119:11(KJV)

Psalm 119:11 reminds us that when we have God's word hidden in our heart, we have less chance of sinning against him. When we take the time to learn the word for ourselves, we have a better grasp of it which helps us not to sin against God. Again, the enemy comes to steal, kill, and destroy, so he wants to make us question what God's word says so he can destroy our future.

3. Be ready when temptation comes. Matt 4:1-11

Then Jesus was led up by the Spirit into the wilderness to be tempted by the devil. ² And when He had fasted forty days and forty nights, afterward He was hungry. ³ Now when the tempter came to Him, he said, "If You are the Son of God, command that these stones become bread."

⁴ But He answered and said, "It is written, 'Man shall not live by bread alone, but by every word that proceeds from the mouth of God.'"

⁵ Then the devil took Him up into the holy city, set Him on the pinnacle of the temple, ⁶ and said to Him, "If You are the Son of God, throw Yourself down. For it is written:

'He shall give His angels charge over you,' and,

'In their hands they shall bear you up, Lest you dash your foot against a stone.'"

⁷ Jesus said to him, "It is written again, 'You shall not tempt the LORD your God.'"

⁸ Again, the devil took Him up on an exceedingly high mountain, and showed Him all the kingdoms of the world and their glory. ⁹ And he said to Him, "All these things I will give You if You will fall down and worship me."

Daughters Of The Most High

¹⁰ Then Jesus said to him, "Away with you, Satan! For it is written, 'You shall worship the LORD your God, and Him only you shall serve."
¹¹ Then the devil left Him, and behold, angels came and ministered to Him.

Matt 4:1-11 (NKJV)

As I briefly mentioned earlier Jesus was tempted during a very weak moment, but He knew the word of God. It was hidden in his heart so He was able to use it as a weapon against the enemy. Satan came to destroy Jesus' future and ours and Jesus was ready to fight the word of the enemy with the Word of His Father. Jesus didn't let his flesh dictate His faith and to be honest the devil was offering some pretty good stuff. Bread when He was hungry, power when He was feeling weak, and the opportunity to test God with misplaced faith. Jesus could have easily given up but He knew that over 2000 years later we would need Him to have been sinless up on that cross. He didn't just think about himself but about what his sin would do for the rest of us. We need to be ready in the same way. When we know His Word for ourselves and hide it in our heart, we will be ready for the temptation that comes our way. We will be able to give the word right back to the enemy and not back down. Eventually the enemy will flee… just like he did with Jesus.

4. Stay in constant fellowship with God.
John 15:7

⁷ If you abide in Me, and My words abide in you, you will[a] ask what you desire, and it shall be done for you.

John 15:7 (NKJV)

Had Eve been abiding in God and had she went to Him first, she wouldn't have been looking to fruit to give her what God was capable of blessing her with. God would have explained to her what He meant when He said certainly die. She would have been able to ask him what wisdom was about and if He would increase hers. She would have been warned about the wiles of the serpent and would have been able to avoid the costly mistake. Well the same applies to us. We have the opportunity to commune with God on a daily basis. We don't have to wait until Sunday to talk to God or hear His Word. We don't have to wait for the preacher to get our healing, we can pray for ourselves. God's Word says if we abide in Him then we can ask for what we desire and it will be done for us. All it takes is us making sure we keep our relationship going with God and we can ask for what we will. So when the enemy comes along trying to convince us of anything different, we already know not only is he probably not telling the truth but God can give it to us shame, guilt, remorse, and sin free.

Why God still loves Eve

Because we've all been a little Eve'ish at one point or another. We have listened to the word of the enemy over the word of God. We believed when people told us we were something that we were not or even that we weren't something that we know God's word has called us to be. We have let our eyes lead us and walked by sight and not by faith. We have also had moments when we thought we were as wise as God, thought we knew better than His word said. Just like Eve, we fell for the lies. We should forgive Eve because we should forgive ourselves. Yes we've made mistakes and our decisions have cost us and others at times, but guess what. God still loves you. He didn't kill Adam and Eve because of their indiscretions. No, He punished them but He still provided. He didn't send them out into the cold world all alone. He clothed them and placed them. He didn't stop talking with them. Did their relationship change, of course it did, but He didn't abandon them. The blessing for us is that we are covered by the blood of Jesus. Our mistakes may hurt at the time and may even disappoint others but guess what 9.5 times out of 10 it didn't kill us, it taught us and made us stronger.

Mrs. Lot

We Can Learn a Lot from Mrs. Lot

²⁶But Lot's wife looked back, and she became a pillar of salt.
Genesis 19:26

Here we have Mrs. Lot. She is the wife of Lot, Abraham's nephew. The highlight of her story is when we find her and her family being faced with imminent destruction. God was set to destroy the place in which the Lot family called home. The angels instructed Lot to take his daughters and wife to a nearby city. They were given the simple instruction to not look back, but to run to safety because God was about to destroy Sodom and Gomorrah. This is where we learn it doesn't take a lot of mistakes to ruin your life… just one.

Mrs. Lot's Smart Move

Mrs. Lot's smart move was following her husband and the angels. It sounds as though there was a choice. Mrs. Lot could have chosen to stay with her daughters that stayed with their husbands. Based off of verses 12-15, it sounds like the Lots had 2 daughters still living at home and some daughters that were married. Lot went to petition the son in laws to leave but they didn't take him seriously. So in verse 15 the angels said take your wife and the daughters HERE and leave. So in theory I believe Mrs. Lot could have said "I can't leave my daughters, I'm going to try to convince them" and ran in the other direction. However Mrs. Lot decided to be obedient and follow her husband.

Mrs. Lot's Not So Smart Move

As I stated in her intro, Mrs. Lot made one dumb move... she looked back. Now in her defense, the consequence was not laid out for her like they were for Eve. The angels just said don't look back. Nobody ever stated she would turn to salt. It doesn't say why she looked back either. Was she like most of us... just nosey?

Make it plain, illustration break

Let me take a moment to tell a little story. So I was "dating" this guy. I use the term dating loosely. I was openly 1 of many women. Now I was the lucky one to be the only one he was intimate with (lucky me... I know right). It would have been an ideal situation if my heart and the Holy Spirit hadn't reminded me I was worth more than just an occasional date and the title of "Main friend with benefits." So God began to move me out of the situation and guess what analogy He used... you guessed it, Sodom and Gomorrah. No lie, I was sitting in service and the guest preacher came over where I was and I promise he looked at me and said "Nakilah... (Ok so he didn't call me by name but he might as well

Mrs. Lot

had) God is trying to destroy Sodom and Gomorrah and he can't because you're still there!" Imagine my conviction since God had already used this illustration! The guest preacher was doing to me what the angels were doing to Lot and his family, basically dragging me out because I was too dumb to leave on my own. So like Mrs. Lot, even though I had left the "city" I was still very, very, tempted to look back. To see just how God was going to destroy the city. So I can understand the spirit of "Nosey", and that spirit almost took me out! I blocked him on social media and deleted his number so I wouldn't be tempted to call. Then one day there he was… I see him out. Now I'm looking and smelling good and I have his attention. He hugged me and then pulled me closer and says I should consider unblocking him on social media. There it was the temptation to look back, to not go totally back in the "city" but to play on the outskirts. I said I'd think about it and took one more sniff of his cologne because he was looking and smelling good too. I had to attend our 2nd service at church that day and we had a guest preacher. In the middle of his sermon he deviated from his message and says " I normally don't use my gift like this but to the woman who is thinking about bringing him back into your life, don't do it. God said he's not done bringing him down and He can't if you're there!" I kid you not and I have the audio to prove it. So he was just like the angel warning me not to look back. I didn't ask any question, I immediately dismissed the idea of bringing him back in my life. That word was just for me, no doubt about it. It was not meant for me to be able to see the destruction first hand; I just had to believe that God had it covered. Speaking of covering as I write I realize that God really loves me. He could have let me be destroyed with the other women who stuck around. But He didn't. He couldn't even begin His destruction until I moved. Wow! How amazing is our God and His love for us. Back to Mrs. Lot.

Mrs. Lot's Not So Smart Move

Maybe she wanted to see what the destruction looked like. Again, we really don't know why she looked back. Maybe she was missing those she left behind. Maybe since the consequences weren't clearly stated she didn't realize the danger of looking back. Unfortunately she did and when she did the punishment was instant. As nasty as the place sounds you would think that she didn't want to look back, maybe it was a guilty indulgence, a place where there is a feeling of not being judged for what we like, but praised for the naughty things we expose. We would think that she would head for the hills and not care, but maybe she had been there so long that she developed a sense of connection with Sodom and Gomorrah. Yeah there were tons of sexually sinful acts going on, but maybe at night as she look out her window she could see the pleasure and passion as two men engaged in their sexual act. Maybe she could hear the moans of pleasure as the men laid with the female prostitutes. Maybe she heard Drake when he said "this stuff is as fun as it looks" and she found herself intrigued with the naughty activities. Maybe she got caught up in the secret fantasy of it all. Maybe they all had just a little bit. It does say that the angels not only warned them but had to pretty much drag them all out the city. What was the hesitation? I can only speculate but can I be honest, sometimes we find ourselves in places we know is wrong, but it feels so good indulging in the desires of our flesh. When God was calling me out of the "city" what do you think I missed…our exciting conversations? Of course a little but I also missed the pleasure I found. I missed the pleasure and the physical satisfaction. I missed the freedom of being explore my guilty pleasure. Is this too real for you? I hope not, because it's real life. Most of us won't admit it either. We stay in situations that are clearly wrong for us but because we love the pleasure and want to avoid being alone. We say it's because we love the person but the truth is we love the physical pleasure. Mrs. Lot came from a Godly family. Her uncle in law was Abraham for goodness sake, The Father of the Promise. She had walked and talked with Abraham I'm sure. So we can safely assume she's a "good girl" and we all know that good girls don't do "bad things" or so we are taught. So was the taboo of the naughty city a reason she looked back. We can only imagine.

Lots of Lessons from Sister Lot

1. Regardless of what others do, follow where the Word of God leads you. If He loves you enough to move you, then move!

2. Realize that everything the Lord asks you to do is for a reason, even if a clear consequence isn't stated. Jeremiah 29:11 reminds us that God has plans to prosper and not harm us. So even though He does not give us full disclosure he gives us the command, for a reason. There are amazing things God wants to do with my life, some things I know and some I don't, but I know they are amazing. There was no way God was going to be able to bless me living in the "city" I was in.

3. No matter how tempted we are we can't look back, because death could come to us just like it did for Sis. Lot. It may not be physical/ it can be spiritual, mental, or emotional. Unfortunately sometimes it is

physical. Going back to an escalated physically abusive relationship can bring about actual death. If you have a sister friend or you yourself are in this situation please be the angle and pull her out. If it's you please find a local resource to assist. It will not get better. We can also look back to a situation and die other types of deaths; deaths of our self-esteem, of our confidence, of the trust of others have placed in us. There is also the death of friendships as well. In my situation had I gone back, there would have been all kinds of things dying inside of me. One of the women who looked back, she and I had formed a friendships. She let the allure of the "city" cause her to turn around and in that moment our friendship died and some of my respect for her did too because she allowed his lies to overrule God's word. Sound a little like Eve huh. People had been praying for her, speaking life into her, encouraging her and she let all that die for whatever her reason for looking back was. She made that choice and it left her feeling salty... pun intended. So we may not know exactly the danger but know that there is danger and looking back should not be an option.

Why God Still Loves a Lot of Us.

Even when we've been foolish enough to look back God still forgives us. Do we suffer the consequences? Yes but grace, mercy and forgiveness is still given Romans 5:20 reminds us that where sin increases, grace increases all the more, but it also reminds us that it's not a ticket to sin. We may not get the full brunt of the punishment but we are often still left feeling salty when we go back to situations God has pulled us from. The beauty in all this is the very thing I discovered while writing, that God loved me enough to pull me out! He even loved me enough to warn me in the middle of a sermon not to turn back. He knew the "death" I would face, He knew what drama would lie ahead. The Lot family faced even more drama after Mrs. Lot turned around.

How Can We Avoid a Lot of Drama

We can trust God. We can trust He bought us out for a reason, trust His instructions and not question. We should trust that He's working all things out for good and has plans to prosper us. We have to learn to TRUST God. He sits high and looks low, so please believe He sees the WHOLE picture and not just the little part we see. We are to keep moving forward and not look back. Yeah we are to be the salt of the earth (Matt 5:13) but remember God's plans never leave us feeling salty.

The Lot Ladies

A Lot More Lessons from the Lot Ladies

Genesis 19:30-38

[30] And Lot went up out of Zoar, and dwelt in the mountain, and his two daughters with him; for he feared to dwell in Zoar: and he dwelt in a cave, he and his two daughters.

[31] And the firstborn said unto the younger, Our father is old, and there is not a man in the earth to come in unto us after the manner of all the earth:

[32] Come, let us make our father drink wine, and we will lie with him, that we may preserve seed of our father.

[33] And they made their father drink wine that night: and the firstborn went in, and lay with her father; and he perceived not when she lay down, nor when she arose.

[34] And it came to pass on the morrow, that the firstborn said unto the younger, Behold, I lay yesternight with my father: let us make him drink wine this night also; and go thou in, and lie with him, that we may preserve seed of our father.

Daughters Of The Most High

[35] And they made their father drink wine that night also: and the younger arose, and lay with him; and he perceived not when she lay down, nor when she arose.

[36] Thus were both the daughters of Lot with child by their father.

[37] And the first born bare a son, and called his name Moab: the same is the father of the Moabites unto this day.

[38] And the younger, she also bare a son, and called his name Benammi: the same is the father of the children of Ammon unto this day.

Just when we thought we had learned so much from Mrs. Lot we find ourselves looking at the Lot daughters and discovering so much more! The Lot girls are briefly mentioned in 2 instances in Genesis the first in 19:6 when their father Lot is offering them up to an angry vicious sexual mob. He is telling the angry mob to spare the angles but do as they please with his daughters. This is a very hard scene to fathom, a father offering up his virgin daughters to an angry mob of sexual predators. Let's pause right here. Am I the only one who finds this utterly and disturbingly disgusting? First Lot you settle your family in a sexually immoral place like Sodom and Gomorrah, a place chosen because it was well watered. So he chose a place with his livestock in mind but not his family so he's raising his family in a place that is full of sin but very profitable. Everyday his precious daughters are surrounded by sexual predators and morally perverse men and women. Just as Mrs. Lot may have become caught up in the pervasion of Sodom, I'm sure his draughts began to be distracted by the perversion as well. How did they feel to hear their father offer them up to the angry mob? What could that have possibly done to their self-esteem? Here we have 2 young ladies with serious daddy issues and trust me we're going to see the fruits of the decisions that their father made on their behalf.

Let's make it personal. This isn't for everybody, but I'm going to bet I'm talking to some very smart women who may have some very serious daddy issues. You can relate to the Lot sisters because your father also made some decisions based off of his financial desires but didn't have you in mind when he made them. Maybe he found the streets and the fast money to be more enticing than being a father, or maybe he chose his own comfort over yours. So you know what it is like for your father's actions to lead you to a place that's morally degrading. Maybe your father has offered you up to this sexually perverse immoral world, allowing it to do to you whatever it pleases. Maybe he didn't offer to send you out to the vicious mob, but he left you alone in this hard cold world. He left you looking for love in all the wrong places and out here to defend yourself against men who want to do with you as they please. It may not look just the same but the concept and consequences are still the same and we can see very similar results. Some smart women doing some very dumb things. The good news is God won't leave us here feeling the hurt of our daddy issues. Hang tight with me and let's hear what the Holy Spirit has to say.

So the second time we see them before we got to the heart of their story is when the angel is pulling them out. Genesis 19:16 says Lot lingered so the men (the angels) took them all by the hand and pulled them out so they could flee. Again daddy Lot is not showing great leadership here. He's lingering but it took the angels pulling them out. Again the Lot girls are right there witnessing it all. They are hearing the angels speaking of destruction, seeing their father hesitate and noticing that it takes someone else to save them. What I'm trying to do here is set the tone for their mindset before we get to the heart of their "not so smart move." Let's look at the men they have for examples.

1. Daddy Lot

He's brought them to an immoral and sexually filthy place. He has made a decision of their living arrangements based off how well watered a place was or how it will be beneficial to his business, but did not consider the sinful nature and what it may do to his family. If this book was about "righteous men who do dumb things" I'd go into more detail about Lot but since it's not we'll just say he may have reverenced God, but he sure didn't think twice about the choices he made for his family.

2. The men of Sodom and Gomorra

All day long the Lot girls experience the men of the town. I'm sure there was always something deplorable going on. So they see men that may not understand the concept of respecting women. Men who only cared to satisfy their flesh in spite of the damage they may cause those involved. These were the men who were constantly around the Lot girls.

3. The Angels

This is the one time we see a positive example for the Lot girls. Now I'm not saying their dad was all wrong. His connection with Abram was enough to cause him to be spared by God per Abram's request, but he clearly lacked proper parenting skills. It was the men of God, the angels that pulled them away from destruction. My hope is that this one act was enough to help convince the Lot girls that there were still some good men around.

Now that we have established a little of their background let's look at

The Lot Girls Smart Move

The Lot girls have quite a few smart moves. Their first smart move just like their mother's was leaving the town about to be destroyed. Now I'm sure they could have objected to leaving but they didn't. They followed their dad to the town of Zora. They also avoided turning back around for their mother. Everybody makes their own choices and we can't keep turning around saving those that can't be saved by us. They also THOUGHT they were making a smart move by coming up with a master plan for survival once they reach the cave their father led them to. Now let me explain a little more background. Lot had asked the angels to spare the town of Zora for him to flee to. The angels granted Lot this request. Instead of staying in Zora where he was supposed to he became afraid that it would be destroyed as well and fled to a cave. How many times have we done this; ask God for something and He grants the request and then we let fear talk us out of our blessing. We ask for the relationship and when God bless us with it we begin to talk ourselves out of it. We ask for the job, God blesses us with it and then we become afraid that we're not good enough to do the work. If we ask God and He says yes, no one can mess that up but you. Don't let fear keep you from enjoying your blessings. Lot's move leads us to the girls coming up with a plan that leads to ...

The Lot Girls Not so Smart Move

Now again I'm not trying to put all the blame on Daddy Lot, but his actions caused big problems, by moving the girls from the town to the cave it gave the girls the impression that there were no more men around. Had Lot been obedient, the girls would have seen the other towns' people and would have not felt they needed a plan. So the older girl tells the younger they will get their father drunk and then take advantage of him and have a son. They execute this scheme and both become pregnant by their father. Their descendants were the Moabites and the Ammonites, who were also enemies to the children of Israel.

Lots Of Lessons From The Lot Sisters

There are so many lessons we can learn from these two. Let's start at the older sister leading the younger sister. We see the older woman misleading the younger women based off of their misconceptions. So because older sis looked around the cave and saw a lack of available men, she suggested and executed a plan for them to share the one man they did see. Hmmmm, this is sounding more and more familiar and common place and we see this every day; women looking around and believing that there are no more eligible men around so we settle with whose available even if we are sharing with our sister. We rationalize our behaviors based off what we see and don't take the time to trust God or investigate. How do I know they didn't take the time to investigate, they didn't consult their father. If they had, Lot would have explained to them that there were still good men out there. He would have told them that they were just in a place of protection and eventually he would lead them out of the cave and they would find a place where they could settle and there would be men to be their husband. Instead, they didn't, they never consulted with the father about their fears of the unknown. They never included the father in their masterplan for matrimony. So my question is have you consulted the Father? Fear is **F**alse **E**vidence **A**ppearing **R**eal and it will make you look at your present relational situation and begin to rationalize foolishness. Fear will cause us to bypass the Father and consult with women in the same situation as us. Fear makes you believe there are no more good men available and it makes more sense to share the men we do see because it's easier to understand. We have to consult the Father when it comes to our master plans on matrimony, if not we'll end up in a major mess.

Another lesson we can glean from the Lot girls is priorities. All hell is breaking loose and the world appears to be falling apart around them. They are living in a dark place out of fear and their main concern is a man. Here they are unsure of where their next meal is coming from and they are worried about finding a man and having a baby. We see this all the time. Women who don't have anything established for themselves but they are chasing behind a man. She doesn't have a steady place to stay, yet she's running behind a man who lives with his momma or baby momma for that matter. I've been there done that and have the t-shirt. You know the type. She's worried about clothes, shoes, and going out to impress a man but don't have a good job or any future goals set but keeps a date. These choices display a clear lack of priorities and the sisters had this issue. What good would it have been to have had children with no real help to raise them? They were plotting to have a baby by a man who had no intentions of being their baby daddy. Man we could just fill one book alone on this topic. Women using any means necessary to have a child by a man who has no desire to father their child, all because she has a false impression that it will solve her issues. The truth of the matter is it only creates more problems. Again their priorities were not aligned with their current situation.

There are a set of daughters that come to mind who when faced with an uncertain future took a different approach. In numbers 27:1-4 we see 5 sisters with their priorities in order. Moses was dividing the land among the different tribes. During this process he was approached by the daughters of Zelophehad. Long story short their father had died with no sons to carry on the family name and receive the inheritance. Instead of going off and trying to find husbands in other tribes and lose their father's rights, they made a very bold and smart move. They approached Moses and with an eloquent argument, secured land under their father's inheritance. They realized they had a choice; let life happen to them and lose out on their promise or come up with a master plan that honored him and secured the future of their sisters. As sisters this is something we should do, worry about securing our future, instead of worrying about getting married as a solution to our problems.

The Lot Ladies

Why God Still Loves A Lot Of Us

Unlike the Lot girls and mother we can recover from our dumb moves. Unless it results in death we have another chance of getting it right. Let's look at where the girls went wrong in order to get it right.

1. Didn't consult the father. As we discussed earlier the ladies didn't discuss with their father the true nature of their circumstances. We all have a limited view on life, even those of us that think and dream big, we still have a limited view. Our Father sits high and looks low, He is everywhere at all times and knows all. None of us can say the same about ourselves. So what we need to learn to do is consult the Father before we make a major life decision. Especially those made from a place of fear. With fear we can't think, hear or even see clearly. Although Lot was operating from a place of disobedience and fear he still was operating a plan that was designed to protect his daughters. Jeremiah 29:11 reminds us that God has plans for us. Plans to prosper us and not to harm us. So again, had the Lot girls reached out to the father first, they would have learned that things weren't as bad as they seemed and that the Father was working on their behalf. This same applies to us. We must reach out to our Heavenly Father first.

2. Matt 6:33 states that we need to seek ye first the kingdom of God and all these things will be added. There are so many scriptures that encourage us to trust God, His word and His plan for us. This trust is built by developing our relationship with our Heavenly Father. Given the issues the Lot girls had with their father it's clear to see there was no solid connection. Had their relationship been stronger he wouldn't have offered them to an angry mob, moved them to the cave in disobedience and they wouldn't have violated their father for their own selfish needs. The good news for us is we have a loving heavenly Father that cares for us and desires to grow closer to us daily. Once this trust and relationship grows we will be less likely to make discussions based off of the misinformation given by fear. We will seek the counsel of the Father

3. Getting our priorities straight. Another lesson we can learn from the Lot girls is having our priorities in order. As I stated they were worried about having a man and a baby when they should have been in survival mode. They should have been working on a plan with their father instead of against their father. So what are your priorities looking like during your current season? Is your money funny but you're still at every party or functions or buying everything you see? Are you having issues with your children or home life and you worried about what some guy is doing on social media? Maybe you're in a dead end job and instead of signing up for school you're too busy watching reality shows and the drama going on in the neighborhood? No matter what your season may be if you are not working with the Father to better your situation than your priorities are definitely in the wrong place

4. Bonus Lesson! Something I haven't touched on with the Lot girls is you have to be careful where you get your advice from. Not everyone who appears to be knowledgeable is, and if it's not backed by the word of God you shouldn't consider it. Anything not supported by scripture is nothing but opinion and someone's opinion has no power in your life. Lil sis Lot took the poor advice of Big sis Lot. She trusted her word because it sounded good even though it wasn't grounded by the Word. In Big Sis defense she was working with limited info as well. She was making what she thought to be the best decision with the information given. Then with her misinformation she led a sister astray. Then the children they birthed the Moabites and the Ammonites were idol worshippers and introduced the children of Israel to some of the most despicable false gods they had known. These two groups of people, the Moabites and the Ammonites, were also enemies of Israel. So we can see how making decisions based off of bad info cannot just harm us but those who are following. We also see how following bad advice can change the direction of our lives. As women taking advice from other women in so many different areas, we must be careful of what we're gleaning from others. Psalm 1:1a reminds us that "blessed is the (wo)man that walks not in the counsel of the wicked…" even though some people may believe they are giving us great advice, if it's not grounded in the Word of God, it may be bad advice. Now Big Sis Lot was not intentionally giving wicked advice but she did. With that, we have to be careful what we say and tell others. We have to make sure were not working as an agent for the enemy.

Why God Loves A Lot Of Us After Big And Small Mistakes

God knew we were imperfect creatures. He knew that we would never be perfect. That's why He sent Jesus. Jesus is a clear indicator that God loved us beyond our mistakes, even when we make a lot of problems and big messes for ourselves and others, God still loves us. God knew from the Garden there would be issues; from Eve believing the enemy's word over God's word, Adam being persuaded by Eve to eat the fruit when he knew better, God knew we would put our fears first when we shouldn't. God knew that we would follow unsound counsel even when we know better and that we would make decisions based off of what we think instead of what our faith knows. God forgives us even when we couldn't forgive ourselves. The Lot girls' story ended shortly after their big mistakes. The world continued to go on. I never read they were killed for their indiscretions so that leads me to believe that a lot of mistakes can be forgiven and we can overcome them. Now what I will mention is that there children suffered greatly for their indiscretions. Their nations were very wicked people. They worshipped false gods that they introduced to the children of Israel and were enemies to the people of God. So just like Lots decisions negatively affecting his children, their decision had negative impact on their children. The Lot family reminds us that our decisions don't just affect us but others as well. We can't just assume that our decisions affect only us. Let's look at this just a little deeper. The Lot girls make their decisions from the desire to have a man. They didn't think about the consequences of their actions. The same thing happens when we make decisions about men and don't consider the outcome. It can have an affect on our children. The choice we make can send our children on the wrong path and a life without God. The good news is God is not only ready to forgive us, but also ready to bless our children. We just have to repent of our sins and trust in the Lord. We have to earn and look to Him even when our world is crumbling down around us. God will lead us in the right direction. He will also take care of our children as well. He wants to see us successful as any good father would.

Leah

Leah's Low Down Love

Genesis 29:10-12, 15-29

[10] When Jacob saw Rachel, daughter of his uncle Laban, and Laban's sheep, he went over and rolled the stone away from the mouth of the well and watered his uncle's sheep. [11] Then Jacob kissed Rachel and began to weep aloud. [12] He had told Rachel that he was a relative of her father and a son of Rebekah. So she ran and told her father. After Jacob had stayed with him for a whole month, [15] Laban said to him, "Just because you are a relative of mine, should you work for me for nothing? Tell me what your wages should be."

[16] Now Laban had two daughters; the name of the older was Leah, and the name of the younger was Rachel. [17] Leah had weak[a] eyes, but Rachel had a lovely figure and was beautiful. [18] Jacob was in love with Rachel and said, "I'll work for you seven years in return for your younger daughter Rachel."

[19] Laban said, "It's better that I give her to you than to some other man. Stay here with me." [20] So Jacob served seven years to get Rachel, but they seemed

like only a few days to him because of his love for her. ²¹ Then Jacob said to Laban, "Give me my wife. My time is completed, and I want to make love to her."

²² So Laban brought together all the people of the place and gave a feast. ²³ But when evening came, he took his daughter Leah and brought her to Jacob, and Jacob made love to her. ²⁴ And Laban gave his servant Zilpah to his daughter as her attendant.

²⁵ When morning came, there was Leah! So Jacob said to Laban, "What is this you have done to me? I served you for Rachel, didn't I? Why have you deceived me?"

²⁶ Laban replied, "It is not our custom here to give the younger daughter in marriage before the older one. ²⁷ Finish this daughter's bridal week; then we will give you the younger one also, in return for another seven years of work."

²⁸ And Jacob did so. He finished the week with Leah, and then Laban gave him his daughter Rachel to be his wife. ²⁹ Laban gave his servant Bilhah to his daughter Rachel as her attendant. ³⁰ Jacob made love to Rachel also, and his love for Rachel was greater than his love for Leah. And he worked for Laban another seven years.

In Genesis 29, we are introduced to a story of 2 men and 2 women and a crazy situation. If I hadn't read this story myself I would truly believe it was the storyline to a Lifetime Original. We are introduced to the Laban girls and a jacked up situation their father put them in. Once again we see a father putting his daughters in compromising positions due to his own greed and deception. So we see how the story goes. Jacob was in love with Rachel and worked 7 years for her. Daddy

Leah

Laban tricked him on the wedding night and gave him Leah instead then gave him Rachel and made Jacob keep them both.

Let's look at big sis, Leah, and talk about the obvious first. She was the less attractive sister. Obviously, this effected several areas of their life. Being the less attractive sister affected her love life. I'm sure her sister, Rachel, had more interest from the men. Jacob fell in love with her on sight but in order for Leah to get married trickery had to be involved. I'm not sure if Laban felt sorry for Leah or if he loved her so much that he wanted to make sure she wasn't left out (which is still feeling sorry for her). Maybe he felt there would never be a suitor for her and so this was her "big chance". His true reasoning isn't quite clear to me. Although he gives the excuse of it not being customary for the older to marry first, we know it was ill intentions because if that's how he truly felt he would have stated that before Jacob agreed to work seven years for Rachel. Whatever the reason, it had to make Leah feel some kind of way about herself and the situation. Here is her obviously more attractive sister and she has a man willing to work and wait seven years for her. Now let's be real. How many of us have found men who are willing to work (court us properly) and wait (no sex) for seven days let alone seven years even though they are deeply attracted to us physically? Verse 11 says when he kissed her he wept loudly and that was just from a kiss. Can you imagine what his body was feeling or saying? We meet a guy and within seven days he's already trying to invite us over to just "kick it" and get our goods. Jacob respected the process of getting Rachel and we should be respected in this same manner as well.

Now I'm not saying we should expect someone to court and wait for seven years, but he should be expected to actively date us and wait for sex until it is right and according to the Word that's marriage. We've seen women like actress Meagan Good and singer Ciara openly express they were waiting until marriage for sex, and from the articles it was the man's decision. By society's standards those are some beautiful women and so was Rachel and there they have men willing to wait for marriage for sex.

Leah's Not So Smart Move

This is exactly where Leah made her first dumb mistake. Leah let her father talk her into sleeping with a man who didn't even like her let alone love her. He offered his daughter up to a man who didn't have her best interest at heart; sounds like Lot, huh? I know the fathers were the head of the household and maybe it's my 21st century feminist side speaking, but could Leah have spoken up for herself and explained to her father that it wasn't right? That Jacob was her sister's husband and that she would just trust and believe God for a husband? Instead, she went along with the plan and had the nerve to say to her sister during an argument "wasn't it enough that you took away MY husband?!" (V 30:15) Wait a minute Leah, since when was he ever really **YOUR** husband. That comment lets me know she had bought into the foolishness her father had put into motion.

Ok, now let me bring this home a bit. Before we get into the many other shenanigans that take place between these two sisters, let's address this major issue; Taking our sister's man, especially the married ones. As Daughters of the Most High, we should never be so desperate to have a man that we resort to sharing/ taking someone else's. We should have this strict girl code that

Leah

states that we ban together and respect their relationship even when he doesn't. What would happen to relationships if we decided we would no longer be the other woman, side chick, homewrecker, or secret lover? What if we held our brothers accountable to their relationships? Guess what, we may never know because we live in a society where we not only don't respect, and won't respect another sister's relationship, but we applaud and celebrate the disrespect. We have songs about it. My favorite of all time is "As We Lay," by Shirley Murdock. She talks about how they forgot about tomorrow, and how she never wanted to hurt his woman, but she (his woman) wouldn't understand how she's feeling about him. We have hit shows that are centered on this disrespect. Let's look back at one of America's favorite shows, Scandal. It is highly popular and the hottest relationship on there was between a married man and his mistress and we LOVE IT! We love the drama, we love the scandal. We idolize a mistress. She's a side chick and a home wrecker, but we don't see her like that. We see her as fierce, strong, successful and a woman who is deeply in love with a man, who just happens to be married. Usually we don't see that as an issue. We dog his wife for not being able to fulfill his needs. This is a problem within our sister society. We allow ourselves or our sisters to become side women and then have the nerves to act Leah'ish by feeling as though this other woman's husband actually belongs to us! I will give it to Jacob, he was not happy with Laban's shenanigans. He did not want Leah nor was he looking to be deceptive. Laban is representative of our girlfriends and society who encourage us to be the other woman and to disrespect the sanctity of someone else's marriage. I could go on and on about this but let's be clear on a few things.

Daughters Of The Most High

1. Being the side chick is not hard. It requires laying down your dignity, pride, morals and your body. You are not special, just easy.
2. He's not going to leave his wife or significant other. He complains because he knows you're gullible enough to buy it. If she was that bad, frigid, evil, trifling, etc. (fill in the blank with any foolish lie you desire) he would have walked away regardless of the cost. This leads me to the 3rd point.
3. She's not as bad as he says. If she is mean and bitter, guess what, it's probably because she is in a relationship with a liar and cheater who is taking her love and heart for granted. If you've ever been cheated on you can relate to her. The pain and agony you felt. The embarrassment and how foolish you felt. You remember how hard it was to walk away because your love and pride wouldn't let you. Take a minute right now and think about all the things you felt when you

   a. Had a suspicion you were being played.
   b. When you were working harder than the FBI to catch him and gather evidence.
   c. When it was finally confirmed and you were faced head on with the truth and afterwards, he did his very best to convince you of how crazy and insecure you were.

Think about it. The hurt and pain. Go ahead. Now you know how she feels. He's told her she's crazy and insecure. She's trying to jump through hoops and work more to recapture his heart while also trying to find out

Leah

the truth. She's hurt, confused and her heart and mind doesn't know which way to turn; no wonder she's mean and bitter. Remember there are 3 sides to every story; his, hers and the truth. So here is our sister hurt and being played and his side chick is being praised because she's cool with expecting less, don't mind keeping his secret, and will give him his way even if it's wrong. She also lies to herself and says she doesn't want more. She acts like "it is what it is" and she's just trying to get hers. Yes, there are a few select women who only want to get serviced in the bedroom and want nothing more than that. In reality, most women want a relationship that consists of dates, and long nights and early mornings; Overnight stays and holidays with the family. Whether it's you or a friend, it is time for the lying to stop! No one really wants to be the sidepiece and if they do its only because they don't love or have any respect for themselves or their sisters. I've been on both sides of the fence and neither is something I'd want any other woman to feel.

Back to the Laban sisters, Leah had the nerves to feel that Jacob really belonged to her and that there was not an issue with her current situation. It's clear that her self-esteem was low and that's why her child count was high. This brings us to her next big mistake. Having babies to keep a man or gain his love. Although Jacob didn't love Leah it surely didn't keep him from getting to know her in the biblical sense {that's my fun way of saying he had sex with her}. Since they had sex on the first date, getting together was nothing new. I'm sure Jacob felt that since he's now responsible for Leah, he might as well enjoy the benefits. It was very obvious that Jacob had no love or desire for Leah. He was visibly upset by the trickery. Verse 30 states that Jacob loved Rachel more than Leah. The very next verse says "when the Lord saw that Leah was hated" which leads me to believe that it was very obvious that Leah was not loved. How does that make her feel? To know that her father put her in a situation where she was not loved and appreciated and it was obvious to everyone around that she was not his first or really second choice.

We should never put ourselves in a position to be a consolation prize. Verse 31 said the "Lord saw she was hated so he opened her womb". I just learned something very valuable, did you catch it? I'll repeat it. "The Lord saw she was hated so he opened her womb". Did you catch it that time? No, that's ok most of us don't. Even though Jacob hated Leah, he was still sleeping with her anyway. It wasn't like he just kind of didn't like her, he HATED her but he still had sex with her. Getting a man to have sex with you is not a magical feat. Also it doesn't mean he loves you, let alone, likes you. Sex for some men can be purely physical. He can have absolutely no emotional ties to the woman he's sleeping with. As women, we have to embrace this truth and stop lying to ourselves or letting our sister friends lie to themselves. There is freedom in knowing the truth. While we're giving all our good stuff away he's on the other side of town trying to build a life with another woman he truly loves. Jacob loved Rachel and he could have had sex with Leah and made love to Rachel. After the Lord opened Leah's womb, she bore a son and called him Reuben and said, "NOW my husband will love me." Now what's wrong with that statement?

> 1. We see that she was well aware of how Jacob really felt about her but she was still holding on to the lie that eventually he would change.

Leah

2. We see that she assumes a son will do the trick. How many women do we know had babies because they assumed it would keep a man in their lives? So, now they've brought a baby into all the foolishness. Now, not only will she find herself being rejected but her baby could have been rejected as well. Leah didn't stop with just Ruben but next came Simeon and she declared that "because the Lord has heard I'm hated, He has given me this son, also."

Now let's take a think break. God saw and heard she was hated and gave her sons. She didn't ask Him but it was what he did for her. I don't believe it was the Lord's desire for her to even be in the situation in the first place. She was in the midst of foolishness created by her father and supported by her actions and He still saw fit to bless her even in the midst of it all.

God knows everything. He knew that those babies wouldn't cause Jacob's heart to change. He did know it would give her hope and lead her to where she needed to be and that was giving Him praise which didn't happen right away. Leah had yet another son named Levi. By son # 3 she thought "Now this time, my husband will be attached to me". How frustrating is it to be in a relationship of sexual convenience. By 3 sons, after at least 27 months (9 mos. per child) Leah is still not loved, still hated, still unattached and still having sex with Jacob on a regular. Wait Leah, you know he don't love you. You know he actually hates you and has no real attachment to you but you are still having sex with him??? Sister, sister, sister what's wrong with you? Whoa…before we start throwing stones at Ms. Leah, let's make sure we don't have any sins… So none of us have met a man and he clearly said "he wasn't looking for a relationship right now and just wants to be "friends" and you gave him the cookie anyway? Telling him you're not really looking for anything serious either and could get with the idea of "friends", but in your mind you believed that if he spends enough time with you, and that he's never had a cookie like the one your serving up, and you'll change his mind. Let's be real. Then we get mad because he only wants you as a friend with benefits. I've seen it happen too many times. Heck, I've done it too many times and I've never won in that situation and neither has any of my sisters who lived that lie. We have to trust God for our own man. One who loves and respects us.

    I want you to put this book down, hop in your car and go to the nearest car dealership. I want you to walk up to the sales person and say, "I want to drive this nice car but I have no desire to commit to an agreement. I don't want to make regular payments and honestly won't make a down payment. I won't fill out any of your paperwork and if I feel like it I will put gas in it and wash it every now and then, but if I don't feel like it you can't do anything about that. I will come and drive it when I want, how I want, and I expect you to be ok with it because I am a nice person and I might possibly think about buying it a few years from now, if I haven't found a better car in the meantime." I then want you to catch an attitude when the salesman asks, "Are you under this same type of agreement with anyone else?" Now that sounded absolutely ridiculous didn't it? When a man approaches you looking for a "friend" with benefits we giggle, feel special and think it's cool, maybe not you but your friends.

    When men say that, they are essentially saying the same thing as the auto scenario. I want to use you when

Leah

I want, how I please with no obligations. I won't even promise consistent dating, and I want you to be "ok" with it, and keep it on the down low. Also, don't question what else I got going on, just stay in your lane. When we agree to being a friend with benefits we are selling ourselves short, while hoping to be chosen. It rarely works out and usually what happens is they end up with the woman who didn't settle for less and held herself to a higher standard. Go back to the car example. Now, imagine what you would think if the dealer looked at you with all seriousness in their eyes and then threw you the keys… happily, excited even. Then begin to show you all the bells and whistles and how everything worked. They even encouraged you to ride it like you owned it (pun intended). Wouldn't you be suspicious? Wonder what's wrong with it and why they are cool with this ridiculous arrangement. Would it keep you from driving it? No, you would ride it until the wheels fell off, but you would have little value in it because you have little invested in it. That's how we do. We gladly give our number, answer booty calls, tell them where all our bells and whistles are and even brag about it. They accept it because who wouldn't want to be with a quality woman, with little to no commitment? Again, nothing is invested so they use and abuse you until there's nothing left and then go invest in a woman who valued herself and her body. That's where our dear Leah found herself. She was a booty call with the title of "wife" or "wifey" for modern day lingo. Eventually, she caught on and I did too. I hope you have as well.

Daughters Of The Most High

Why God Still Loves Us

After 3 pregnancies with the 4th she said, "NOW I will praise the Lord", and she finally got it. Sometimes, it can take us a few knocks upside the head before we realize where our real focus should be. The woman's study bible states it best, "she could not change Jacob, but she could change herself and recognize God's hand in her life." God gives us free will to make our choices and with good choices there are good consequences but with bad choices there are bad consequences. That's when grace and mercy walk in. God knows we are flawed in our thinking and ways. He knows we will make mistakes. Here's Leah, with a man, who's technically hers but he hates her. She's already unattractive and now she's unloved and unattached. She's in this position not because God put her there but through choices made from free will. Of course it was set into motion by someone else, but even Leah begins to buy into the lie. God still blesses her and shows her love. 29:31 stated that He saw she was hated so he (God) opened her womb" this has a 2 part purpose.

1. It made her feel loved at the time.
2. The fact that she was still rejected shows us that even when we get what we think we want, it still may not be the best thing for us. God allowed baby after baby and it wasn't until Judah (4th son) that she realized that it was God who deserved the praise and not Jacob.

An added benefit was now there was someone to love Leah, her sons. I'm sure she found joy in being their mother even if her heart wasn't in the right place to start. Here's the real blessing, her fourth son Judah is the lineage in which the Messiah came! The 3rd son Levi is where the lineage of the priesthood came from. So even in "mistakes" there can be blessings. God still loves us when others don't. Even when we're rejected, God will use us for His glory. Praise God for that revelation!

Why You Should Forgive Yourself

As I write, I'm being slapped all in the face. It was difficult seeing me in Leah. Happily being the side chick and also the "friend with benefits". That closet doesn't just have skeletons but warm bodies. It wasn't that long ago when I was throwing the keys of my heart to men who wanted to drive but not commit. The enemy was in full swing trying to talk me into not finishing this book. Trying to make me feel convicted, but I knew I couldn't quit because God said you needed to hear this and you needed to forgive yourself and move on. We make mistakes, everyone does, now get over it. You can either let it convict and condemn, or you can let it set you free and help someone else in the process. You've done it, now own it, learn and grow from it, and move forward. God can cleanse you, clear out your closet and use your mistakes to bless someone else (Judah and Levi). No mess is too hard for God to clean up. Now remove yourself from the side chick society and take your rightful place as a Daughter of the Most High and purpose in your heart to bring some sisters out with you.

Rachel

Really Rachel

Now let's look at Rachel, Leah's sister. So far, it looked like she was winning in a sense. She had a man work seven years before he could even be with her and then after the deception, he agreed to work seven more years for her love. We struggle getting 14 dates and here she got 14 years of working for her love. She has beauty, Jacob's true love and dedication. I'm sure she was showered with gifts and was given the best treatment. We know this woman; it may describe some of us; beautiful, successful, and the attention and affection of a man or men. Other women want to be her. We see women like this and assume everything is perfect. Rachel helps us understand that is the furthest thing from the truth. Chapter 30 starts with "Now Rachel saw that she bore Jacob no children, Rachel envied her sister…" wait now wait. Really Rachel, you are jealous of poor Leah? The only way she could get a man was to trick yours? She's unattractive, unattached, hated by her husband, mistreated and defeated in love and you are jealous? Well before we prepare to pull the speck out of her eye, let's grab our mirror and make sure there are no planks in ours (Matt 7:5). God can bless us with the sun, moon, and the stars and we can see a sister with one little planet and cry and pout about not having one ourselves. Rachel was crying about a baby, but we can fill so many other things in to fit that scenario in our lives. Promotions, relationships, weight loss, weight gain, better clothes, better shoes, house... you name it we can be jealous and complain about it. This is a problem, once the green eyed monster of envy starts to show up, all reasoning goes out the door. That's exactly what happened to Rachel. The enemy had been sitting on her shoulder talking in her ear. "Look at Leah and her lazy eye. She's not even as pretty as you and God is showing her favor. Does Jacob love her more? Look how many sons she has. He STAYS in her tent. Why hasn't Jacob given you a baby yet? Why does Leah get all the love? Look at her throwing it in your face by flaunting her sons around... what are you going to do about it?" So this is causing Rachel to fill with emotions and anger. At this point, rational behavior is out the window. Can you prove it by the Word Nakilah? I'm glad you asked. Verse 30:1 states "she said to Jacob, "give me children, or I shall die!" O.K. sis, I see a few things wrong with this statement and they confirm that logic has left the building and kicks off Rachel's not so smart moves.

Rachel's Not So Smart Move

First she goes to Jacob demanding HE give her a baby. Now Jacob has waited seven years and one week to be with Rachel and even agreed to work another seven years just to have her. So it's hard for me to believe that he's not sleeping with her on a regular and doing his best to get her pregnant. Having a child, especially a son, is important and, as much as Jacob

Rachel

loved Rachel, I know getting her pregnant was on the top of his list. Rachel is now in her emotional state and is now blaming the man she loves, and who loves her, for what she doesn't have. She's asking him for something only God can do. Hmmmm... sounds familiar. We look to another sister in a relationship. She looks so happy on their FB (Facebook) page, vacations and dates. They look like they are living the dream, she looks so happy. Now the devil is talking in your ear. "Look at her. She's happy because she has a man. If you get a man, you'll be happy, too. I know you wanted to "wait on God" for a mate but you deserve to be happy now. God is trying to keep you from being happy, too. You deserve to be happy; more than she does so go get you a man." So now you go out and get just any kind of man to fill this space and he's not equipped to give you what you need. It's a space that only God can fill and you're mad at this man because he can't make you happy. Just like Rachel was envious of Leah, now you are envious of your sister in Christ and neither you, nor Rachel is taking into account the things your sister had to go through to get to where she is. Rachel failed to remember that Leah was having babies to gain the love she (Rachel) was getting freely. Leah was hated and unattached and her option or "golden ticket" was to have a baby. She was a "wife" by title but not by love. She was settling to be a baby momma when she should have been a wife. Rachel is a wife jealous over a baby momma.

We don't know what our sister had to go through to get to the relationship she now has; the time she may have spent on her face before God, or if she may have gone through physical abuse. She may not even be happy as she's perceived to be. She may look happy online but who's to say that she's happy offline. You have to be careful letting the green eyed monster of envy, and the enemy, put you in a place of irrational thinking. Listen to Rachel talking about "give me children, or I shall die!" Really now Rachel, is it that serious? All that she had from Jacob and this one thing was worth dying over? Before we judge, we do the same thing. God provides all the blessing and we find that ONE THING we feel we can't live without and then act like it's the end of the world. Rachel should have been going to God, with a humble heart, asking Him to bless her. So with this statement, she's gotten Jacob upset with her because she's asking him for something only God can provide. She has allowed jealousy to cause an issue with her man over a woman he doesn't even love or want to be with. Now, she's green with envy and he's red with anger.

This is where Rachel made her next mistake. Jacob replies to her, "am I in the place of God?" and instead of her going to God she comes up with the plan to have him sleep with her servant to conceive a child with him. Now Jacob set out to marry one woman and is now on woman #3, and of course he's not going to turn it down, he's a man. So now he's producing children with his true love's servant and she (Rachel) is claiming the children as her own. So with the first child she claims that "God heard her cause" and had given her a son. Rachel, when did you ever take your cause before God? Do you remember hearing her talk to God? I don't either. Therefore, I'm glad she's giving Him glory, but I don't necessarily see Him confirming her plans. Verse 7 said Jacob went into Bilhah again and produces another son and this time Rachel declares, that after "great wrestling with her sister, she has prevailed." Now, we see Rachel's irrational truth. She wasn't "having a baby" by Jacob because she loved him and wanted to give him a son, but she did it to get back at her sister. Leah had just gotten to a place where she was at peace with God. Giving Him

Rachel

praise, no longer worried about what Jacob was doing. She was minding her own business and wasn't thinking about Rachel. Rachel is messing up her good thing with Jacob. Burning with envy, bringing other women into her marriage to satisfy an already happy husband, and bringing more children into her mess, all the while "blaming" it all on God (thanking him for the babies by the other women when it wasn't His original plan to begin with). What a mess you've created Rachel all because you're jealous. Now how many times have we got with men, started a partnership, made a purchase, etc., and haven't bit more consulted God but acted like He's the one that orchestrated it all, yet it's nothing but foolishness. 1 Corinthians 14:22 reminds us that "God is not the author of confusion but of peace..." and this situation along with some of the mess we find ourselves in, "blaming" God when it was not His doing; allowing, but not His doing. So when we start making moves that appear to be working, but not aligned with the Word of God, we have to be careful to not put the "blame" in the wrong place, because when the foolishness hits the fan, which it always does, we will then put the blame and the anger towards God when it wasn't His "fault" in the first place. We can thank God for the mercy and grace that keeps our dumb moves from not taking us out.

Now, Rachel's actions and jealousy has not only brought more children, women and drama between her and Jacob, she's now pulled Leah back into all this mess. It's been at least 18 months since Leah's last child, she's got her praise, and she's not tripping on Jacob. I can imagine Rachel sashaying through with her new babies. All proud of what she did. I'm sure she made sure to parade around Leah to make sure she saw her new sons and talk about how much their daddy loves them. This leaves Leah feeling some type of way. So instead of staying in her place of praise and peace with God, she starts back playing the Jacob game. She gives her maid Zilpah to Jacob to bear a son. She claims that a troop has come… sounds like "this means war" to me and then Zilpah has another son. Now, Jacob has 4 women and 8 sons. None of the sons were truly conceived out of the love of a husband and wife, but from a desire to be loved and jealousy. Man, if this doesn't sound like modern times; women fighting over a man who, technically, only wants one of them and several children being conceived with the hopes of keeping a man. Leah and Rachel have taken the focus off of God and Jacob and have made it into a battle between the two for them. They are competing with each other over the love of a man and jealousy of wanting what the other has. It's one dumb move after another and unfortunately, they aren't done yet.

    Rachel's next not so smart move happened over some food. So Leah's son Reuben was gathering mandrakes during harvest season. Mandrakes are like a potato and were believed to be an aphrodisiac and have fertility powers (Women's study bible pg. 46). Rachel goes and asks Leah for some of her son's mandrakes. Leah gets smart with her and makes a deal, the mandrakes for a night with Jacob. Now, the Women's Study Bible notes that Rachel is still trying to use trickery and magic rather than asking God for what she wants. She agrees and Leah takes Jacob for the night. Leah met Jacob coming from the field and said, "You must come into me for I have surely hired you with my son's mandrakes." So Jacob is getting "hired out" for food now? Leah, why are you paying for companionship? Well are we going to be the pot or the kettle, because we have done the same thing too… paying for companionship, paying bills, "helping out" putting money on the books,

Rachel

the list goes on and on. Some of us have been guilty of this same thing, paying for dates just so we can have one. No judgement Leah... No judgement.

Now, they are treating Jacob like a trophy and not a husband. Jacob slept with Leah and God heard her and she bore another son. This time she proclaimed God was rewarding her for giving Jacob her servant to sleep with. Now, I'm going to come back to this in just a moment but please believe it's a major lesson here. Leah gets pregnant again and proclaims that God had presented her with a precious gift, and now her husband would honor her because she's had six sons. We thought Leah had learned her lesson, but she was back to her old ways, all because Rachel started taunting her. We never know what our sister has gone through to get to the place of peace she is at. When we operate in jealousy we can set her back. On the flip side of that, we have to mature to a place where we can pause and try to see why someone is behaving the way that they are. Rachel was jealous and her jealously was hurting Leah. If we are Leah, instead of hurting back, we need to remember that Rachel may be hurting too and pray for restoration instead of plotting for revenge.

Notable side lesson

In regards to both women giving their servant to Jacob to stay in competition with one another, I've done some research and still haven't found anything that states God was pleased with this behavior. My point to this is when you know you are operating in foolishness, just because you APPEAR to be getting what you want, doesn't mean God is supporting your decisions or that He is pleased. There is God's perfect will and His permissive will. His perfect will is when we are following

His commandments and living our lives according to His will. We're not perfect but we are living more like Christ. His permissive will is when He gives permission for things to happen even if it's not the best choice. All of the women we have discussed so far were operating in His permissive will, Eve eating the fruit and giving it to Adam to eat. God's perfect will was for them to live in the garden and never have to endure the punishments of sin. His permissive will allowed them to do it, but as always, there are consequences. We all have free will. Although God wants us to make the right choices, He still gives us permission to choose our own path. Leah and Rachel were operating from their feelings. Leah was feeling rejected and yearning for love from Jacob. Rachel was feeling like she was in competition with her sister. They were making babies, not out of love, but from their own ill motives. God used these same children to build a nation. They all represent the 12 tribes of Israel. God says ALL things work together for our good (Romans 8:28). So even though we've made mistakes from our ill motives, God's grace can save our situations. God can take our mess and use it to bless someone else. The children we created from relationships that were not pleasing to God, but will still be used for His glory. God still loves us in spite of us, even when we've pulled others into our mess (the servants), He can still bless us. We just delay those blessings and increase our problems when we don't submit to the PERFECT will of God from the start. So, stop competing with your sisters and trying to find love in all the wrong places, submit to God, check your motives before you make a move, and thank God for his grace and mercy that's bringing you through.

Rachel

Why God Still Loves Us

In verse 22 something amazing happened. God remembered Rachel and God listened to her and opened her womb. Now, there are more than a few good reasons to shout here.

1. Rachel finally took the time to talk to God. It doesn't say when or what she said but she must have come to her senses and asked Him to open her womb. It had to have been previously because to remember something means it happened in the past and you are now recalling it. So at some point she spoke to God and He listened to her and gave her what she desired. Maybe it wasn't a direct request. Psalm 37:4 reminds us that God knows the desires of our heart. So maybe He heard her heart's desire or a simple prayer that she whispered.

2. Not all prayers are answered right away. We have to be patient and allow God to do what He is going to do. Rachel was anxious because she saw her sister with what she wanted. Instead of waiting on God, she did her own thing. We've all been Rachel. I remember one day we were enjoying a Sunday outside. We had the grill sizzling, music playing and the lawn chairs out. It started to sprinkle and we said a prayer, kind of tongue in cheek, asking God to stop the rain. We then started moving the stuff into the garage. A few minutes later the rain stopped. I told my mother and my daughter "God said why ask for something and then expect that it's not going to happen just because it takes minutes to manifest." That day we learned to expect our prayer to be answered even if it doesn't happen

right away. Don't ask for something if you're not going to give Him time to do it or expect that He will.

3. Delayed doesn't mean denied. Rachel had asked for a child but her actions said she didn't expect for it to happen.

4. God remembers you. It may not feel like it but God has not forgotten you. If we prepare for the blessing and expect God to deliver, we can be ready when "yes" finally comes. I'm waiting on a few "finally" blessings myself. Rachel should forgive the fact that she was impatient and you should too. She should also forgive herself for being jealous of her sister. It's human nature. We see what we want and we want it right then, and if someone else has what we want, they become our secret enemy. God was not going to forget about her or you for that matter. The blessing was definitely delayed but far from denied. Rachel gave birth to Joseph, who was his father's favorite and an important figure in the bible (Story begins in Genesis 37). No matter what we're waiting on; Ask, Seek, Knock (Matt 7:7) and be patient enough to wait for the door to open.

Sarah

Sarah's Swayed Faith

Genesis 18:1-5, 10-15

The L‍ord appeared to Abraham near the great trees of Mamre while he was sitting at the entrance to his tent in the heat of the day. [2] Abraham looked up and saw three men standing nearby. When he saw them, he hurried from the entrance of his tent to meet them and bowed low to the ground.
[3] He said, "If I have found favor in your eyes, my lord, do not pass your servant by. [4] Let a little water be brought, and then you may all wash your feet and rest under this tree. [5] Let me get you something to eat, so you can be refreshed and then go on your way—now that you have come to your servant."
"Very well," they answered, "do as you say."
[10] Then one of them said, "I will surely return to you about this time next year, and Sarah your wife will have a son."
Now Sarah was listening at the entrance to the tent, which was behind him. [11] Abraham and Sarah were already very old, and Sarah was past the age of childbearing. [12] So Sarah laughed to herself as she

thought, "After I am worn out and my lord is old, will I now have this pleasure?"

¹³ Then the LORD said to Abraham, "Why did Sarah laugh and say, 'Will I really have a child, now that I am old?' ¹⁴ Is anything too hard for the LORD? I will return to you at the appointed time next year, and Sarah will have a son."

¹⁵ Sarah was afraid, so she lied and said, "I did not laugh."

But he said, "Yes, you did laugh."

Here we have Sister Sarah. She is married to Abraham who is the Father to the nations. So this makes her a mother to the nations. Sarah is faced with a highly unusual announcement. There are 3 visitors that come and visit with Abraham and give him the announcement that this time next year Sarah would have a baby. Sarah hears this and laughs and says "after I am worn out and my lord is old will I now have this pleasure." Basically Sarah is saying "Really God, after all this time NOW you want to bless me in this area?" The visitors reply, "is there anything too hard for God?" and then confirms that when they return next year Sarah will have a son. In her embarrassment Sarah lied and said she never laughed but the visitor called her out on it. Sarah is given a revelation and due to her lack of faith she laughed. To be honest most of us would too. There are some blessings that we just give up on. If I was 90 and someone came and told me I was going to have a baby, I would not only laugh but throw in a "You must have lost your mind!" We find some revelations to be downright comical. Not because its laughs of joy but laughs of disbelief. This is where Sarah finds herself. Wow lets step back real quick in Genesis 17:17 Abraham receives this same revelation a second time from God. He did the same things, except he fell down laughing, and this was from God directly! So when the visitors talked to Abraham it was confirmation, but Sarah still found it comical. Also let's look at the 3 visitors. This is what's called a theophany. A theophany is a visible manifestation to humankind of God (Google), so basically Abraham and Sarah were visited by God. It starts the chapter saying that the Lord came to visit Abraham. So anyway you look at it this is a direct revelation from the Lord and they still laughed.

Before we judge Sarah about her lack of faith we've done the same thing. God could have said "Go back to school" and instead of running out to sign up for classes we laugh and say "Yeah right, I'm too old to go back to school." Maybe God wants you to start a business or ministry and you laugh and say were not smart enough or make enough money. We can receive a revelation and let our faith waiver just like Sarah. I love the reply of the Lord. He challenges Sarah with the question of "Is there anything too hard for the Lord" and that's my question for you today. "Is anything too hard for the Lord?" He's created the whole world and you are tripping over a bill or feeling kike he can't help you obtain a degree or even have a baby. Nothing is too hard for God even when it's hard for us to believe.

Sarah's not so smart move

Sarah's' not so smart move happened a few chapters back in chapter 16. Sarai (her name at the time) became impatient with waiting for a child. She proposed to have her Egyptian slave Hagar bear a child by Abram (his name at the time) to build a family. Now God had said **Sarah** would have a child and not by proxy. Abram received this promise in Genesis 15. So between chapters 15-16 Sarah moves before God and organizes Hagar having the baby and then between chapters 16-19 she has lost all hope in bearing her own child. There are a few issues with Sarah. She took matters into her own hands and didn't wait on God. She knew that God was going to make a nation out of her offspring but didn't give God time to move. We've seen this time and time again. We make this mistake often in our relationships and finances. We hear God saying He will bless us with a great relationship but we keep settling for knuckle heads. We try to take matters into our own hands and date anybody who looks good. We also make moves with our money without consulting with God. We make major purchases without consulting God. He wants us to be financially stable but refuses to let Him handle our money. This is where Sarah made her first mistake. Having a promise of God but not giving him the opportunity to fulfill it HIS way. I've made this mistake far too many times.

The next issue was Sarah doubted God's ability. Sarah's wavering faith was an indication that she doubted the power of God. I always like to say if it makes sense it don't make faith. The beauty of God is that He handles the impossible in our lives. He specializes in the supernatural. All we have to do is believe. Like Sarah, sometimes we hear a promise of God and we have a hard time believing. We look at our current situations and allow what we see to dictate what we believe. This is a big mistake. The very definition of faith is the "substance of things hoped for, the evidence of things unseen" (Hebrew 11:1). When we have faith in something we begin to act in a way that backs up what we believe. If we have faith that God will work out a situation then we stop worrying and start making necessary moves. Let's think about an example in the Bible. The woman with an issue of Blood (Luke 8:43-48)

Sarah

is a good example. She had been bleeding for 12 long years. She had spent her money going from Dr. to Dr. trying to find a cure. Her faith led her to Jesus. She believed if she just touched him that she would be healed. When Jesus realized it was her he said to her "daughter your faith has healed you." She believed, moved on that belief; it worked out for her benefit and she received exactly what she needed. That's what Sarah should have done. When the visitor (Lord) said this time next year when we return she would have a son, she should have ran and started preparing a nursery. Any Google search will show you several scriptures where God said he would provide and hear our prayer when we move by faith. There should be no doubt in our mind that God can and will do it. God has shaped a universe, created man from dust, parted a red sea; surely, Sarah, he can give you a baby and surely sis he can meet your needs too.

Next on the "not so smart" list is when she lied to the Lord right there in His face. He's God and knows and sees all from the heavens, surely He sees and hears when He's standing right there. Maybe it was out of embarrassment or shame, but I'm not sure why she lied to God. What I do know is we shouldn't do it. We have to be honest with God and honest with ourselves. We're having a hard time believing we must simply be honest with God. When we are totally transparent we open the door for our faith to grow. Remember God knows you inside out when we are honest with him, we're honest with ourselves.

The list keeps growing as we talk about yet another not so smart move from Sarah (Are you keeping track?). She blamed Abraham for HER decision in getting Hagar pregnant. In Genesis 16:2 it says Sarai came up with the plan and Abram agreed to what she said. Then when she starts to feel Hagar is mocking her she is fussing at Abram saying he is "responsible for the wrong she is suffering." So how can you blame him for your great plan failing? It was her bright idea and he did what he thought would satisfy her. Abram does what Sarah told him to do, get Hagar pregnant, now she begins to regret the decision. It's not fair for us to make hasty or not so smart moves, and then look to blame others when things go wrong. It's not right when people do it to us and it sure isn't right to do it to others or God for that matter. We discussed that with Rachel and Leah, making plans and then saying it was God's doing in the sense of approval. When plans go wrong then guess who we would blame? That's right, God. Here Abram is getting the punishment. Once again to appease her he says for her to do to Hagar as she will.

Sarai makes another wrong move by treating Hagar so bad she wanted to leave. Hagar never asked to be in this position; it was Sarah who brought her into it. We should never treat our sister bad due to something we did wrong. That is pride and there is no room for that in the Kingdom. We have to take responsibility for our actions and whatever consequences they produce. Sarah allowed her insecurities and impatience to put a sister in a bad place. As we learned with Leah and Rachel, dragging other sisters into our mess is always a big mistake. If we're doing our part; seeking God, godly counsel, not making decisions based off our feelings, we wouldn't have to worry about hurting others in this manner. I know we jumped around with Sarah but her not so smart moves transcend chapters. Honestly so does ours. We cause unnecessary chapter delays because we fail to obey God from the beginning. Trust me I know.

Sarah

Why God loves us through the laugh

Sarah's wavering faith caused her to laugh at the plans God had for her. You've waited until I'm old to FINALLY want to bless me. Even with her attitude, God still blessed her. Genesis 21:1 says "Now the LORD was gracious to Sarah as he had said, and the LORD did for Sarah what he had promised. ²Sarah became pregnant and bore a son" Sarah and Abraham are the parents to many nations. God did it in their old age but He still did it. God isn't moved by time the way we are, everything works in seasons. Ecclesiastes 3:1 reminds us that there is a time for everything, and a season for every activity under the heavens." Your age doesn't worry God nor does your financial status, education level, career, background or any previous circumstance. He moves in seasons and uses whom He pleases. I'm a single mother of 3. God didn't worry about my background or bank account but looked at my heart. The way society feels about me doesn't deter God either. He is only concerned with my level of faith in His Word. He has called me to do some radical things. There are people who are far more qualified than I am and God is still trying to convince them to write a book, start a ministry, run a business or go share His Gospel. We have to get to a place where we have "Crazy Faith" as I like to call it. God should be able to call us to do the unimaginable. When we surrender to God and begin to move eventually we will begin to see how everything comes into play. For God to get the glory, He has to write the story. Here's an example. One year for the toy drive I handled 20 kids. So the next year I figured we'd step it up a little and do 40 but one of my board members began to question my decision. I had enough faith to believe that if God gave me the vision He would grant the provision. I encouraged her to stretch her faith. As the drive went on more and more kids began to come and the donations were not keeping up. I had an amazing opportunity to be a featured charity through a local radio station. Normally people are bringing donations by the truckloads but just the opposite happened for me. I received $20.00 and 11 more children trying to get on my list. I felt so defeated. The ones on my team who didn't believe 40 children were possible were waiting to see me fail. I cried and prayed and wondered if I had missed God. I was lying in bed in tears and the phone rang. I had been dogging calls all day but God said to answer this one. It was a local cell phone company that heard me on the radio and was willing to sponsor a whole family! After that the blessings just flooded in. it was nothing BUT GOD! That year I ended up helping over 80 kids! God showed my naysayers that not only will He match my desire but do exceedingly and abundantly above what I asked! That experience not only increased my faith and the faith of others, but silenced the enemy as well. If we had the resources to pull it off personally where would God's glory come from? We would take credit for the results. God makes the impossible very possible with a faithful heart.

    God did for Sarah exactly what he said he would do. Even after her faith swayed, he still blessed her. I dedicate this chapter to baby Zoey. She is my best friends "finally blessing" after several attempts to get pregnant and facing 40, God finally blessed her with a baby. He did it in His time and it's perfect. Her life is more settled, she has an established business and her and her husband have their dream home. God did it all in His time, even when she may have given up the idea. I'm waiting for my "finally blessing" in the area of marriage

Sarah

just like many of you. We've endured the crazy men and the heartache and pain of failed relationships. It looks like God has forgotten. We try to take matters into our own hands and fail. Sarah and baby Zoey reminds us that for everything there is a season and purpose, and it is perfect in God's sight. Just like we can't rush winter to bring spring, we can't rush our life seasons to get to another. Patience is a virtue for a reason. God does deliver "finally blessings" and as I anticipate the birth of baby Zoey, I anticipate my "forever blessing" with my future husband and I anticipate the deliverance of your "finally" as well. Whenever we are faced with something we can't fathom or understand, it stretches our minds as well as our faith. Again I ask you, "Is there anything too hard for the Lord?" Absolutely not!

"Be still and know that I am God, I will be exalted among the nations, I will be exalted in the earth."

Psalm 46:10

Tamar

Tamar's Tragic Testimony

Now, I want to make myself very clear before I jump into Tamar's tragic testimony. I am not blaming Tamar. Back in those days women were expected to follow the direction of the men. As we've been reading we can see how the men in some of these women's lives played a very intricate part in their decision making. I will however highlight the lessons we can glean from her testimony.

Here we have a brother named Amnon, meaning "loyal and faithful" in Hebrew. We will soon find he was everything but that. He is sitting around lusting after his half-sister Tamar so much that he's becoming physically sick. She must have been one fine sister. Now incest wasn't acceptable during those times but self-control was the last thing on Amnon's mind. He saw what he wanted and was determined to get it. Listening to a friend, Amnon pretended to be something he wasn't to get his sister in his bedroom. This should start to sound really familiar to you. There are several brothers out there who are pretending to be something they aren't just so they can sleep with you. Amnon's trickery works and here we find Tamar and her cakes in Amnon's bedroom. Now again, we know that Tamar didn't have much of a choice in her going. She was sent by her father to go help her brothers. She was assuming that she was going to be a blessing to him. For the sake of the lessons God wants us to learn we will say that she did have a choice. So she gets word that her brother is sick and he wants her to come to his room.

Tamar's Not So Smart Move

Tamar, why are we not asking more questions? Why does he need ME to come and serve him? Doesn't he have servants? What makes my cakes so special that he needs me to come to his bedroom to make them? Why can't I bake them at my house and drop them off? Tamar didn't ask enough questions. She was headed to a brother's bedroom to satisfy a need she wasn't called to fulfill. She wasn't his wife or his servant. Why are we so quick and willing to fulfill desires that aren't our job? That scripture didn't say "Tamar, who had the best cakes in the kingdom," No, so why was she called to do something that wasn't her role, the same reason we do, because we are being naive. We meet a brother and in no time he's requesting our cakes in his bedroom *cakes is an urban reference to a woman's derriere and a sexual reference.* We have no business with our cakes in his space and neither did Tamar. She was completely unaware of what was about to go down and on rare occasions so are we. There are some of us who know what the deal is. We know he wants sex but like we've been discussing we think that when he get us he will secretly want a relationship. However, there are times we think he is an upstanding good man but find ourselves a victim of date rape.

Tamar

We have to start being more mindful of who we are with and what we are doing. Today most meeting is done online. So we're meeting these men, reading a profile and feeling like after a few chats we know them. Then we're hooking up, hanging out, and putting ourselves in dangerous positions because were not thinking clearly. We're putting ourselves in compromising situations and suffering MAJOR consequences like our sister Tamar is about to experience. Tamar is in the room making his cakes and he clears the room. At this point she should be feeling a little nervous. Surely she had to know a little about his character. He was her brother. Maybe she went off the fact his name means loyalty and faithful so surely he would be loyal to her and she could trust him. I have a feeling that she was pretty comfortable with him because he was her brother and she thought she could trust him. This is where we go wrong as well, we think we can trust him because he's our brother. Our Father is the same so we think we are safe around them but that's not always the case. Even our Christian brothers are capable of devaluing us and putting us in compromising situations. We can't trust or assume that every brother is going to protect us because at the end of the day they are men and have desires like everybody else regardless of what they try to make you believe.

So now Tamar is alone with Amnon and realizes she's in trouble. She tried compromising with him by offering marriage as an alternative and he wanted no parts of that. He wanted one thing and one thing only and that was sex. He was so consumed with lust that he was going through with this deceptive plan to rape his sister. It was pre-meditated and it was going down. He didn't care about hurting her or the disgrace it was going to cause. He knew the law of the land like everyone else and he could have had any other woman but decided that it was his sister he had to have. A man consumed with lust to the point he is ready to rape you has no desire to listen to your reasoning.

This is why we have to be careful of the situations we allow ourselves to be put in. There are **SOME** dumb moves that can cost us far more than we're willing to pay. Next to death this move was paying the ultimate cost. Tamar tries to reason with him. "What about me, where could I get rid of my disgrace?" She even suggested that he speak to their father for her hand in marriage. Amnon was not interested in reasoning. The fact that he didn't agree to marriage indicated he wanted one thing from Tamar and he was strong enough to get it. This left Tamar broken and defeated and Amnon's next move further indicates what type of man he really was. Verse 15 says "Then Amnon hated her with intense hatred. In fact he hated her more than he loved her." How tragic. We meet men like this too. I call it the "Amnon Syndrome" which means before he sleeps with you he desires you with such intensity and once he gets it, whether consensual or not, he begins to hate you more than his desire to have you in the first place. I dated a guy once that told me that if he slept with a woman he had no desire after that to marry her and I knew first hand his pursuit was intense. We see it time and time again, men who just have to have us. They pursue and beg and plead, put on a front, whatever they have to do, even play sick to get a sister to sleep with them and once it's done so are they.

After this tragic act, Amnon keeps pouring the salt on the wound. He tells her to get up and get out and he proceeds to kick Tamar out of his house. Then Tamar makes her next not so smart move. She tells him that kicking her out is worse than what he had just done to her and begs to stay. She was begging to stay in a relationship with a brother that hated her and had no desire to be with her. What a shame, begging and pleading to stay in an abusive relationship like a battered woman who stays with her abuser or keeps going back. It's like they have given up on life and feel that no one else will want them. That's where Tamar was. She knew that since she was no longer a virgin the idea of marriage was no longer an option. Again, Amnon wouldn't listen and he put her out. He had the servants throw her out and bolt the door behind her and they even threw her coat of many colors out. That is what the daughters of the King would wear to show everyone they are still pure and an indication of whom they were. Not only has he tricked her, violated her, but now he has kicked her out. She is broken, full of shame and now abandoned. She is no longer a candidate for marriage because she is no longer a virgin. Amnon didn't care at all about how he left his sister.

I'm trying not to shout because I know what's coming next under the "why God still loves us section. I'm going to try to continue to work out the lessons we learned from Tamar's testimony.

Tamar's Big Lesson

We can't trust every brother just because we have the same Father. I have encountered MANY men in church that were supposed to be my brothers in the faith but their behavior said something different. 2 timothy 3:1-7 is my favorite teaching scripture right now. It first describes perilous times and perilous men; the word perilous means full of danger or risk so it's describing dangerous times and dangerous men. It says they are lovers of pleasure rather than lovers of God and also they have a form of godliness but denying its power (4b, 5). They sit in church every Sunday and they look like family, they look loyal and faithful. We feel as though we can trust them when we are alone with them. Timothy goes on to warn "these are the types that smooth talk (MSG version) themselves into the homes and gain CONTROL of gullible women (NIV). Gullible women (don't take offense, just learn the lesson like I had to and let's grow together). Gullible means easily persuaded to believe something. We have been gullible, easily persuaded even when we thought we were being strong. We thought we had crossed all T's and dotted all I's but somehow still ended up in these dumb situations BUT HOW?!?!? I'm glad you asked.

Smart Girls do Smart Things

1. 2 timothy 3:6b says the woman are loaded down with sin and led away by various lusts. Loaded down by sin. Sin is our past mistakes. So we are still carrying around the mistakes made in the past; dumb things we did back when, are still weighting us down. It's time to let them go! Yes you made mistakes. Yes you did some really dumb things but guess what, God has forgiven you and you need to forgive yourself as well. Worrying about what you did last year, last month or even last night is keeping you down and holding you back. It's keeping you in shame and that shame begins to shape your thoughts about yourself. So now not only are you feeling shame but you're not feeling like you deserve the best. So when one of the smooth talkers comes your way, even though you see

Tamar

some warning signs, you feel this is the best you deserve. If you're dealing with an Amnon and you don't see the danger right away, you're not going to God to hear His voice on the matter. Sin pulls us from the very one who can free and deliver us.

2. Another reason we are easily swayed is because we're led away by our various lusts. Lust is a strong desire for something, usually sex. Remember Amnon was lusting for his sister. So we have these desires we haven't gotten under control through the help of the Holy Spirit. You know the feeling... "I know he's no good but when he calls to come through I just can't help but say yes". We let flesh and desires make our choices instead of consulting God. The sex is so good all reason goes out the door. The money is so good we just can't let go. His compliments are so sweet you can't help but call to hear them. We have our ways of justifying our foolishness just like Leah and Rachel. We know deep in our heart that it's nothing but our flesh and not the favor of the Father. So our lust and our sins are weighing us down and leading us away, neither of these are from God and both can be eliminated if we surrender. We can't afford to keep making dumb moves and as Tamar shows us some of those mistakes can lead to lifelong devastation.

3. Application.

We have to apply what we learn to keep us from these dumb situations. 2 timothy 3:7 "always learning and never able to come to the knowledge of the truth." We can learn and learn but never truly come into the knowledge of what we learned. We don't apply it to our lives. We hear the Word but refuse to be a doer of the word and then wonder why we're going through the things we go through. James 1:22 "But don't just listen to God's word. You must do what it says. Otherwise, you are only fooling yourselves."

Now I'm preaching to myself as well. It wasn't until I stopped listening to my flesh and started listening to the Father that I began to steer clear of dumb situations. In some situations I had to learn the hard way, the very hard way. I wish I had applied what I learned a long time ago. I would honestly probably be married by now and far more financially stable. Instead I allowed my desires to override the voice of the Holy Spirit. Like Eve I found myself believing the word of the Enemy over the Word of God. We have to stop being so easily swayed. Just like Mrs. Lot, God tried to bring her from a place of sexual immorality but she perished due to looking back from the very thing God was saving her from. God is trying to deliver us from the sins that so easily beset us and we keep trying to go back. Back to the sexual sins and other desires that can lead to our destruction. The lesson we learned from the Lot girls reminds us that we need to get our priorities straight. We are worried about a man when all hell is breaking loose instead of talking to the Master about a plan. Also we can't be so quick to believe there are no more good men and make a bad decision, but take the time to explore our options before we settle. Leah taught us that we DESERVE to be loved and that we should NEVER settle for our sister's husband or man. She reminded us that a baby NEVER solidifies a relationship and if we have to scheme to get what we want we will not win in the end. Rachel's jealousy was a lesson about not being distracted by what we don't have but enjoy the blessings of right now. There is also a very valuable lesson that GOD HAS NOT FORGOT. When we take matters into our own hands we move too soon, possibly causing our sisters pain, and create far more drama for ourselves than God ever intended for us to have. Again, Hagar and Sarah teach us the same lesson. Trust God's timing. He knows what He's doing. He doesn't need our help to push along the plan and he doesn't need our input on how it should be done. His word won't return to Him void and it will prosper in what it set out to do. God does it bigger and better than we could EVER imagine. Last but not least our sister Tamar shows us that there are some dumb things we can do that will cost us FAR more than we EVER intend to pay.

Which brings me to the shouting portion. *que the musicians and the organ player and ushers get the white sheets*

Why God Still Loves Us

I think we can all agree that Tamar suffered a terrible tragedy at the hands of her brother Amnon. He used and abused her, and left her ashamed and broken. Her brother discarded her like trash and threw her identity out with her. But Tamar had another brother. His name was Absalom. He took her in and gave her comfort. He also avenged her honor. He told her to hold her peace because he would handle it, and in chapter in verses 23-33 he did just that and Amnon paid with his life for what he had done to Tamar. God told me to tell you that you have a brother who wants to restore you as well. His name is Jesus. He has sent Jesus to take you up when your brothers have forsaken you. Jesus will pay the price for your sins and restore you. Jesus is known as the Prince of peace. Guess what Absalom's name means… father of peace! Tamar's brother's name meant peace and that's what Jesus gives us! He also restores us, avenges us and comforts us when others have done us wrong. We know without a doubt that God loves us because He sent Jesus to be our brother (John 3:16)! I wanted to break out in praise while writing this. No matter what happens, no matter what we go through Jesus is there for us. Promising to never leave or forsake us (Deuteronomy 31:6). Promising to fight our battles and forgive us of our sins (1 John 1:9). Jesus knocks at the door waiting for you to answer (Revelation 3:20). He doesn't want to just give you religion he wants to have a relationship with you. Jesus sat with the sinners because that's who he came for. He doesn't judge who we use to be but is only concerned with where we're going. 2 Corinthians 5:17 "Therefore, if **anyone** {even smart girls who do dumb things} is in Christ, the new creation has come: The old has gone, the new is here!" You have to get to know him for yourself. I had to do that.

My personal testimony

When I got to college I turned my back on Jesus. I didn't want any parts of Him. Due to my lack of knowledge in the Word I felt that it was Jesus fault I wasn't able to be saved. I grew up in a denomination where certain things had to happen before you would be considered "saved" I thought it was Jesus fault (that's another story I talk about in the book "A Woman's Guide to Setting a Blaze in ministry, business, and life") so me and Jesus fell all the way out. I wanted no parts of Him. I tried my best to find another way to God. I studied religion in college and learned all I could about my other options. My life was a living hell. I had no real peace during that time. I was unhappy and even suicidal at certain points of time. Then one Saturday night after I had been caught up in yet another dumb situation, God said "That's enough it's time." I went to church that next morning at my daughter's daycare and I reconnected not just with my Heavenly Father but with Jesus as well. I made Jesus my choice not because of what my mother had done, and her grandmother, but I chose him because I knew without a doubt that He was the best choice. I knew my options and I developed our relationship from a personal standpoint instead of going to church out of obligation or tradition. Nothing else out there was going to do. Not Buddha or Muhammad but Jesus. It was that time I decided that I would believe in the Bible from front to back and have complete faith in its power. No one can convince me that my big brother Jesus isn't real. I know he's real I know God's real. He's done too much for me! I am a smart girl who's done some really dumb things. I'm 99.9% sure I will do some more, but guess what, I know that even in the midst of it all God still loves me and He loves you too! Sis you are forgiven! You are restored and you are a Daughter of the Most High! You are fearfully and wonderfully made. God is not done with you. There is a beautiful next chapter waiting for you if you want it, but you have to trust God. You have to pick up your robe of many colors and find peace in your brother Jesus. You have to forgive yourself and those who played a role in the not so smart moves you decided to make. Sister, rest knowing you are still a Daughter of the Most High God and that God knew you before He formed you (Jeremiah 1:5). Flaws and all he STILL chose you (John 15:16). Now walk in that freedom (John 8:36). Smart Girls do Smart Things and Sister that's you!

Nakilah Shannon

Daughter of The Most High
Minister ~ Author ~ Inspirational Speaker ~ Radio Host

Nakilah is the "tell it like it is" honest girlfriend that every woman needs and can relate to. Her witty delivery style allows the tough issues to be addressed in a manner that makes it easy for her audience to understand and she gives real solutions to their everyday problems. Nakilah is relevant and relatable.

Nakilah is an inspirational writer and speaker who enjoy being a humble Ambassador for Christ. Sharing her testimony and lending a helping hand to other women as well as her community is her life's purpose. Through her leadership and ministry, Hagar's Fountain of Hope Inc, Minister Nakilah meets the needs of local single mothers and women by empowering, encouraging, educating, and edifying them even during the most devastating hardships. As a mother of three, she knows first-hand the difficulties that single mothers face. With a commitment to serve, she offers the community wisdom, encouragement, and supportive resources to help individuals meet their personal goals in life.

7 Days to Pray the Single Away
is a book divinely appointed and inspired by the Spirit of God specifically designed to break the
chains of singleness. Through incorporating the principles of this book and strategic scripturally based prayers for seven days with a prayer partner, you will emerge spiritually rejuvenated and fully prepared for your rightful place before God at the altar.
Available on Amazon
Great for groups and organizations

Speaking Topics
(Not all inclusive):
Girls Night In- 7 Days to Pray event
Single Living
Sisterhood
Empowering and Encouraging Women
Single Mother Issues

Contact Information:
Website: www.hagarsfountainofhope.org
Email:hagarfoh@yahoo.com
Facebook: AuthorNakilah Shannon
Instagram: hagarfoh

www.ingramcontent.com/pod-product-compliance
Lightning Source LLC
Chambersburg PA
CBHW071158090426
42736CB00012B/2367